SERIES

A life-changing encounter
with God's Word from the books of

1 & 2 SAMUEL

A NavPress resource published in alliance
with Tyndale House Publishers, Inc.

NAVPRESS○®

NavPress is the publishing ministry of The Navigators, an international Christian organization and leader in personal spiritual development. NavPress is committed to helping people grow spiritually and enjoy lives of meaning and hope through personal and group resources that are biblically rooted, culturally relevant, and highly practical.

For more information, visit www.NavPress.com.

1 & 2 Samuel

Copyright © 2012 by The Navigators. All rights reserved.

A NavPress resource published in alliance with Tyndale House Publishers, Inc.

NAVPRESS and the NAVPRESS logo are registered trademarks of NavPress, The Navigators, Colorado Springs, CO. *TYNDALE* is a registered trademark of Tyndale House Publishers, Inc. Absence of ® in connection with marks of NavPress or other parties does not indicate an absence of registration of those marks.

ISBN 978-1-61521-734-2

Printed in the United States of America

21 20 19 18 17 16
9   8   7   6   5   4

CONTENTS

HOW TO USE THIS GUIDE

Along with all the volumes in the LifeChange series of Bible studies, this guide to 1 and 2 Samuel shares common goals:

1. To provide you with a firm foundation of understanding, plus a thirst to return to 1 and 2 Samuel throughout your life.

2. To give you study patterns and skills that help you explore every part of the Bible.

3. To offer you historical background, word definitions, and explanation notes to aid your study.

4. To help you grasp as a whole the message of both 1 and 2 Samuel.

5. To teach you how to let God's Word transform you into Christ's image.

As You Begin

This guide includes ten lessons, which will take you chapter by chapter through all of 1 and 2 Samuel. Each lesson is designed to take from one to two hours of preparation to complete on your own. To benefit most from this time, here's a good way to begin your work on each lesson:

1. Pray for God's help to keep you mentally alert and spiritually sensitive.

2. Read attentively through the entire passage mentioned in the lesson's title. (You may want to read the passage from two or more Bible versions—perhaps at least once from a more literal translation such as the New International Version, English Standard Version, New American Standard Bible, or New King James Version, and perhaps once more in a paraphrase such as *The Message* or the New Living Translation.) Do your reading in an environment that's as free as possible from distractions. Allow your mind and heart to meditate on these words you encounter, words that are God's personal gift to you and to all His people.

After reading the passage, you're ready to dive into the numbered questions in this guide that make up the main portion of each lesson. Each of these questions is followed by blank space for writing your answers. (This act of writing your answers helps clarify your thinking and stimulates your mental engagement with the passage, as well as your later recall.) Use extra paper or a notebook if the space for recording your answers seems too cramped. Continue through the questions in numbered order. If any question seems too difficult or unclear, just skip it and go on to the next.

Each of these questions will typically direct you back to 1 Samuel or 2 Samuel to look again at a certain portion of the assigned passage for that lesson. (At this point be sure to use a more literal Bible translation, rather than a paraphrase.)

As you look closer at this passage, it's helpful to approach it in this progression:

Observe. What does the passage actually *say*? Ask God to help you see it clearly. Notice everything that's there.

Interpret. What does the passage *mean*? Ask God to help you understand. And remember that any passage's meaning is fundamentally determined by its *context*. So stay alert to all you'll see about the setting and background of 1 and 2 Samuel, and keep thinking of these books as a whole while you proceed through them chapter by chapter. You'll be progressively building up your insights and familiarity with what they're all about.

Apply. Keep asking yourself, *How does this truth affect my life?* (Pray for God's help as you examine yourself in light of that truth and in light of His purpose for each passage.)

Try to consciously follow all three of these approaches as you shape your written answer to each question in the lesson.

The Extras

In addition to the regular numbered questions you see in this guide, each lesson also offers several "optional" questions or suggestions that appear in the margins. All of these will appear under one of three headings:

Optional Application. These are suggested options for application. Consider these with prayerful sensitivity to the Lord's guidance.

For Thought and Discussion. Many of these questions address various ethical issues and other biblical principles that lead to a wide range of implications. They tend to be particularly suited for group discussions.

For Further Study. These often include cross-references to other parts of the Bible that shed light on a topic in the lesson, plus questions that delve deeper into the passage.

(For additional help for more effective Bible study, refer to the "Study Aids" section starting on page 179.)

Changing Your Life

Don't let your study become an exercise in knowledge alone. Treat the passage as *God's* Word, and stay in dialogue with Him as you study. Pray, "Lord, what do You want me to notice here?" "Father, why is this true?" "Lord, how does my life measure up to this?"

Let biblical truth sink into your inner convictions so you'll increasingly be able to act on this truth as a natural way of living.

At times you may want to consider memorizing a certain verse or passage you come across in your study, one that particularly challenges or encourages you. To help with that, write down the words on a card to keep with you and set aside a few minutes each day to think about the passage. Recite it to yourself repeatedly, always thinking about its meaning. Return to it as often as you can, for a brief review. You'll soon find the words coming to mind spontaneously, and they'll begin to affect your motives and actions.

For Group Study

Exploring Scripture together in a group is especially valuable for the encouragement, support, and accountability it provides as you seek to apply God's Word to your life. As a group you can listen jointly for God's guidance, pray for each other, help one another resist temptation, and share the spiritual principles you're learning to put into practice. Together you affirm that growing in faith, hope, and love is important and that *you need each other* in the process.

A group of four to ten people allows for the closest understanding of each other and the richest discussions in Bible study, but you can adapt this guide for other sized groups. It will suit a wide range of group types, such as home Bible studies, growth groups, youth groups, and church classes. Both new and mature Christians will benefit from the guide, regardless of their previous experience in Bible study.

Aim for a positive atmosphere of acceptance, honesty, and openness. In your first meeting, explore candidly everyone's expectations and goals for your time together.

A typical schedule for group study is to take one lesson per week, but feel free to split lessons if you want to discuss them more thoroughly. Or omit some questions in a lesson if your preparation or discussion time is limited. (You can always return to this guide later for further study on your own.)

When you come together, you probably won't have time to discuss all the questions in the lesson, so it's helpful to choose ahead of time the ones you want to be sure to cover thoroughly. This is one of the main responsibilities that a group leader typically assumes.

Each lesson in this guide ends with a section called "For the Group." It gives advice for that particular lesson on how to focus the discussion, how to apply the lesson to daily life, and so on. Reading each lesson's "For the Group" section ahead of time can help the leader be more effective in guiding the group.

You'll get the greatest benefit from your time together if each group member also prepares ahead of time by writing out his or her answers to each question in the lesson. The private reflection and prayer that this preparation can stimulate will be especially important in helping everyone discern how God wants you to apply each lesson to your daily life.

There are many ways to structure the group meeting, and in fact you may want to vary your routine occasionally to help keep things fresh.

Here are some of the elements you can consider including as you come together for each lesson:

Pray together. It's good to pause for prayer as you begin your time together, as well as to incorporate a later more extensive time of prayer for each other, after you've had time to share personal needs and prayer requests (you may want to write these down in a notebook). When you begin with prayer, it's worthwhile and honoring to God to ask especially for His Holy Spirit's guidance of your time together.

Worship. Some groups like to sing together and worship God with prayers of praise.

Review. You may want to take time to discuss what difference the previous week's lesson has made in your lives as well as recall the major emphasis you discovered in the passage for that week.

Read the passage aloud. Once you're ready to focus attention together on the assigned Scripture passage in this week's lesson, read it aloud. (One person could do this, or the reading could be shared.)

Open up for lingering questions. Allow time for the group members to mention anything in the passage that they may have particular questions about.

Summarize the passage. Have one or two persons offer a summary of what the passage tells us about.

Discuss. This will be the heart of your time together, and will likely take the biggest portion of your time. Focus on the questions you see as the most important and most helpful. Allow and encourage everyone to be part of the discussion on each question. You may want to take written notes as the discussion proceeds. Ask follow-up questions to sharpen your attention and to deepen your understanding of what you discuss. You may want give special attention to the questions in the margin under the heading "For Thought and Discussion." Remember that sometimes these can be especially good for discussion, but be prepared for widely different answers and opinions. As you hear each other, keep in mind your various backgrounds and personalities and ways of thinking. You can practice godly discernment without ungodly judgment in your discussion.

Encourage further personal study. You can find more opportunities for exploring this lesson's themes and issues under the marginal heading "For Further Study" throughout the lesson. You can also pursue some of these together during your group time.

Focus on application. Look especially at the "Optional Application" listed in the margins throughout the lesson. Keep encouraging one another in the continual work of adjusting our lives to the truths God gives us in Scripture.

Summarize your discoveries. You may want to read aloud through the passage one last time together, using this opportunity to solidify your understanding and appreciation of it and to clarify how the Lord is speaking to you through it.

Look ahead. Glance together at the headings and questions in the next lesson to see what's coming.

Give thanks to God. It's good to end your time together by pausing to express gratitude to God for His Word and for the work of His Spirit in your minds and hearts during your time together.

Get to know each other better. In early sessions together, you may want to spend time establishing trust, common ground, and a sense of each other's background and what each person hopes to gain from the study. This may help you later with honest discussion about how the Bible applies to each of you. Understanding each other better will make it easier to share about personal applications.

Keep these worthy guidelines in mind throughout your time together:

Let us consider how we may spur one another on toward love and good deeds.

(HEBREWS 10:24)

Carry each other's burdens, and in this way you will fulfill the law of Christ.

(GALATIANS 6:2)

Accept one another, then, just as Christ accepted you, in order to bring praise to God.

(ROMANS 15:7)

OVERVIEW

THE BOOKS OF 1 & 2 SAMUEL

God's Kingdom Comes

The easily apparent purpose of the books of 1 and 2 Samuel is to preserve the history of God's work in establishing the kingdom of Israel three thousand years ago.

"In the books of Samuel, monarchy becomes a reality. Three dominant figures—Samuel the kingmaker, Saul the abortive king, David the ideal king—highlight its agonies as well as its ecstasies."[1]

"The central theme of the books of Samuel is God's exercising of his cosmic kingship by inaugurating a David dynasty ('house') in Israel (2 Samuel 7; Psalm 89) . . . and by electing the holy city Zion (Jerusalem; 2 Samuel 6; Psalm 132) as the place where David's successor will establish the temple ('house') for the worship of the divine King Yahweh (see 2 Samuel 24:18)."[2]

It's fitting that a work that focuses on such an exalted subject should be frequently read and highly appreciated by God's people, as has traditionally been the case with 1 and 2 Samuel.

A Display of God's Love

The dramatic establishment of this kingdom is a further reflection of God's compassion toward Israel, especially after so many long decades of turmoil in its history.

"The period of the Judges shows the serious problems Israel had, both in its leadership and among the people as a whole. The books of Samuel show God's continued care for his people, in raising up for them a king whose job was to be their champion, representative, and example."[3]

"A major purpose of Samuel, then, is to define monarchy as a gracious gift of God to his chosen people."[4]

Energy and Motion

The story that conveys this larger context of the great new kingdom is a gripping one, filled with striking details and movement. "Sweeping change . . . is a hallmark of the Samuel narratives—change guided and energized by the Lord himself through fragile vessels of the likes of Samuel, Saul, and David."[5]

Authorship

Some scholars believe that the same author or authors may well have composed the books of Joshua, Judges, 1 and 2 Samuel, and 1 and 2 Kings. (In some ancient traditions, the two books of Samuel and the two books of Kings are presented as four parts of the same work.) However, the books themselves provide no clear indication of who their author is. Fortunately, identifying that author is unnecessary for understanding and highly appreciating their content.

Although we don't have an authoritative description of how these books were first written or later arranged—or by whom—in 1 Chronicles 29:29 we read, "As for the events of King David's reign, from beginning to end, they are written in the records of Samuel the seer, the records of Nathan the prophet and the records of Gad the seer." These "records" from the prophets Samuel, Nathan, and Gad may well have formed at least the core of what we know today as 1 and 2 Samuel.

A connection is frequently noted between 1 and 2 Samuel and the Mosaic teaching and perspective in Deuteronomy, which is seen as a dominant theme throughout these books. "The books of Samuel were probably given their final form by someone deeply influenced by the theology of the Book of Deuteronomy."[6]

Taken together, the text of 1 and 2 Samuel has about the same number of words as the later combined books of 1 and 2 Kings or of 1 and 2 Chronicles. Each of these three combined works—Samuel, Kings, and Chronicles—is only slightly shorter than the book of Jeremiah, the longest of all the Bible's books (in terms of total words). So in sheer size alone, the combined work of 1 and 2 Samuel commands a prominent place in the Old Testament and in all of Scripture.

Interpreting Old Testament Narratives[7]

A narrative is a story. When we read a biblical narrative, we are reading part of the true story about God as He revealed Himself to people over the centuries. Here are some principles for interpreting any biblical narrative, particularly Old Testament ones:

1. Not every episode in Israel's history is meant to teach an individual moral lesson. Sometimes a story is significant only as part of the whole history of God's dealings with Israel.

2. Narratives record what happened, not necessarily what ought to happen every time. So again, a particular story may not have its own

---

moral. (For example, the fact that Hannah made a vow to dedicate Samuel may not be a timeless model for barren women.)

3. Not every detail of a narrative has deep significance. (The exact way Eli's sons exploited worshipers probably doesn't.) The point may be in the overall message. However, the point may not be clear until we carefully observe many details. (By comparing the sons' practices to the laws in Leviticus and Deuteronomy, we can see that their behavior violated not just general courtesy but express commands of God.)

4. Narratives often teach by clearly implying something without actually stating it. (We may infer that 1 Samuel 2:18-21 is meant to imply that the Lord rewarded Hannah for her generous gift of her son.) However, we should be wary of teachers who see "hidden" meanings that other Christians do not see.

5. A narrative will never imply something that another passage of Scripture explicitly contradicts or forbids. We use the plain teaching portions of Scripture to evaluate what happens in the narrative portions.

6. "*All* narratives are selective and incomplete. Not all the relevant details are always given (see John 21:25). What does appear in the narrative is everything that the inspired author thought important for us to know." (We must be content with our curiosity unsatisfied about details of Samuel's, Saul's, David's, and others' lives that the Scripture does not give.)

7. "Narratives are not written to answer all our theological questions. They have particular, specific, limited purposes and deal with certain issues, leaving others to be dealt with elsewhere in other ways." (The text doesn't address whether Eli was "saved" or "damned," and we shouldn't speculate.)

8. God is the main character (the hero) of all biblical narratives. The human beings are always secondary characters in a story about what God did.

Applying Old Testament Narratives[8]

Keep the following five guidelines in mind as you seek to apply Old Testament narratives to yourself:

1. What people do in narratives is not necessarily a good example to us. Frequently it is just the opposite (1 Samuel 4:3-4 is an instance of this).

2. Most of the characters in narratives are far from perfect, and so are their actions. This is true of obvious sinners like Eli and great men like David. Thus, we should not try to copy everything even David does. We should let the rest of Scripture, especially the New Testament, guide us in drawing lessons for application.

3. We are not always told at the end of a narrative whether what happened was good or bad. (Was it good or bad that the ark was captured?) We are expected to be able to decide that on the basis of what God has said directly elsewhere in the Scriptures.

(continued on page 14)

(continued from page 13)

4. In every case, God is speaking to and dealing with a particular person (such as Samuel, Eli, Saul, or David). We should not think we are supposed to do everything He tells someone in the narrative to do. (For instance, since He commanded different tactics in almost every one of Israel's battles, we can't assume that we should adopt one or another of those tactics for one of our battles. Samuel's instructions to Saul in 1 Samuel chapters 13 and 15 are also specific to those situations.) Instead of looking for tactics to copy, we should focus on God's character, His aims, and the variety of His methods. We should pray for discernment from the Holy Spirit and uncoerced confirmation from other Christians before we apply a specific command (such as to wait, go forward, or make peace) to ourselves.

5. If God's Word illustrates a principle that the New Testament would uphold, then we can apply the principle to *genuinely comparable* situations in our own lives. Our task is to discern the principle accurately and make sure that our situations are truly comparable. This is not always easy, and it always requires wisdom from the Holy Spirit and guidance from the New Testament. Discussion with other discerning Christians also helps guard against error.

Timeline — From Samuel to Solomon

Birth of Samuel (1 Samuel 1:20)	1105 BC
Birth of Saul	1080
Saul anointed to be king (1 Samuel 10:1)	1050
Birth of David	1040
David anointed to be Saul's successor (1 Samuel 16:1-13)	1025
Saul's death; David begins reign over Judah in Hebron (2 Samuel 1:1; 2 Samuel 2:1,4,11)	1010
Birth of Solomon (2 Samuel 12:24)	991
David's death and beginning of Solomon's reign (2 Samuel 5:4-5; 1 Kings 2:10-11; 3:7; 11:42)	970
Solomon's death; Israel splits into Israel and Judah (1 Kings 11:41–12:24)	930

1. Ronald F. Youngblood, *Expositor's Bible Commentary*, ed. Frank E. Gaebelein, vol. 3, *1–2 Samuel* (Grand Rapids, MI: Zondervan, 1992), 557.
2. *ESV Study Bible* (Wheaton, IL: Crossway, 2008), introduction to 1–2 Samuel: "Theme."
3. *ESV Study Bible*, introduction to 1–2 Samuel: "History of Salvation Summary."
4. Youngblood, 558.
5. Youngblood, 560.
6. *New Geneva Study Bible* (Nashville: Thomas Nelson, 1995), introduction to 1 Samuel: "Author."
7. Gordon Fee and Douglas Stuart, *How to Read the Bible for All Its Worth* (Grand Rapids, MI: Zondervan, 1982), 74–75, 78. Fee and Stuart's book is the source for all the material in this sidebar.
8. Fee and Stuart, 78. Again, this book is the source for the material used in this sidebar.

1 SAMUEL

A Kingdom Born

First Samuel focuses on the dramatic stories of the three central characters in the kingdom's birth: Samuel, Saul, and David. Their stories are filled with triumph as well as tragedy—and their examples offer much for us to learn from.

Along with the purpose of highlighting the kingdom's establishment, "a second purpose of the book is to embody universal human experience as the means of teaching moral and spiritual lessons for all people at all times. Some of the lessons are individual and personal, involving (for example) the specific family situations of Eli, Saul, and David. But others apply to communities and nations, such as the lessons we learn about good and bad leadership for a people as seen in the conduct of Eli, Samuel, and Saul. Presented with such positive and negative examples, we can learn much about our daily lives by reading and pondering the book of 1 Samuel. Because the author is more interested in a few important figures than in groups and movements, we naturally remember the book partly by the characters who remain in our memory, especially Hannah, Eli, Samuel, Saul, Jonathan, and David."[1]

The compelling personalities of these key figures in 1 Samuel draw us into the story to closely observe each of them—for our lasting benefit. "First Samuel is a book of personalities, so paying close attention to characterization is important. Similarly, the book is rich in universal, recognizable human experience, with the result that building bridges between the world of the text and one's own experiences is an inviting approach to the book. Even though this book does not cover the vast spans of Israelite history that the other Old Testament historical chronicles cover, it provides in-depth analyses of what makes for good and bad leadership. What is true for leaders, moreover, is true for all individuals in their choices for or against God. A leading literary purpose of the book is to embody universal human experience as the means of teaching moral and spiritual lessons for all people at all times."[2]

Ultimately—and most profoundly—1 Samuel points us to a future King. "First Samuel recounts the history of Israel at a very crucial stage of its existence. The crucial development in the nation was its unwillingness to have God as its only king. As we observe this phase of Israelite history, we are led to ponder what kind of rule we need and to conclude that only the eventual Son of David, Christ, is sufficient."[3]

1. Leland Ryken and Philip Graham Ryken, eds., *The Literary Study Bible* (Wheaton, IL: Crossway, 2007), introduction to 1 Samuel: "The Book at a Glance."
2. *ESV Study Bible* (Wheaton, IL: Crossway, 2008), introduction to 1–2 Samuel: "Literary Features."
3. Ryken and Ryken, "1 Samuel as a Chapter in the Master Story of the Bible."

1 SAMUEL 1–7

Samuel's Rise

1. For getting the most from 1 and 2 Samuel, one of the best guidelines is found in 2 Timothy 3:16-17, words Paul wrote with the Old Testament first in view. He said that *all* Scripture is of great benefit to (a) teach us, (b) rebuke us, (c) correct us, and (d) train us in righteousness. Paul added that these Scriptures completely equip the person of God "for every good work." As you think seriously about those guidelines, in which of these areas do you especially want to experience the usefulness of 1 Samuel? Express your desire in a written prayer to God.

_____

_____

_____

_____

_____

_____

2. Glance ahead through the pages of 1 Samuel, and look for a recurring theme or thought in each of the following verses: 3:19; 10:7; 16:18; 17:37; 18:12; 20:13 (see also 2 Samuel 5:10; 7:3,9). What is that theme? Why is it important to God, and why is it important for all of God's people in all ages?

_____

_____

Optional Application: We read that after His resurrection, when Jesus was explaining Old Testament passages to His disciples, He "opened their minds so they could understand the Scriptures" (Luke 24:45). Ask God to do that kind of work in *your* mind as you study 1 Samuel, so you're released and free to learn everything here He wants you to learn — and so you can become as bold and worshipful and faithful as those early disciples of Jesus were. Express this desire to Him in prayer.

For Further Study:
The book of Judges gives important background to the events of 1 Samuel. Read Judges 1:1–3:6 (which describes the overall pattern of events during the period of the judges), 6:1-6 (which explains the severity of the foreign oppression Israel suffered), and 19:1–20:48 (which recounts the nation's internal difficulties). What important information do you discover in these passages?

Optional Application: Just as God's presence with David is a major theme throughout 1 and 2 Samuel, so David was able to say to God, "I will fear no evil, for you are with me" (Psalm 23:4). What to you is the greatest indication of God's presence with you? And what to you is the greatest benefit of His presence?

3. In one sitting if possible, read through the first seven chapters of 1 Samuel. What two or three things stand out most to you from your reading?

_____

_____

_____

_____

Hannah and Samuel (1 Samuel 1:1–2:12)

4. How would you describe Hannah's plight, as we see it in 1:1-7?

_____

_____

_____

_____

5. a. In 1:9-11 and 1:15-16, what attitudes does Hannah show toward her situation?

_____

_____

_____

_____

b. In those same verses, what attitudes toward the Lord does Hannah demonstrate?

_____

_____

_____

_____

Ramathaim (1:1). Perhaps another name for Ramah (see 1:19; 2:11). It is probably the Ramah in Benjamin about five miles north of Jerusalem.

Ephraimite (1:1). Since his son became a priest, Elkanah was probably a Levite whose family belonged to the clans that had been allotted towns in Ephraim (see Joshua 21:20-21).[1]

Two wives (1:2). Having more than one wife at once was never the rule in the ancient world, and only kings had large harems. Yet several Old Testament figures, such as Abraham and Jacob, had more than one wife. The reasons for polygamy were more cultural and economic than erotic. When organized government was weak or nonexistent and each family had to care for itself, a large number of children was often considered a necessity. Thus when one wife failed to bear children for her husband, he might take another also (see Genesis 16:1-4; 25:1-4). Even in the case of monarchs, marriages were often more a means of sealing an alliance than anything else (see 1 Kings 3:1). So polygamy, while never God's purpose for the human race, should not be regarded in itself as a sign of immorality.

Year after year (1:3). Every Israelite male was required to attend festivals at the central sanctuary three times a year (see Deuteronomy 16:16-17). Elkanah probably brought his wives to the Feast of Tabernacles, when the nation celebrated God's blessing on the year's fertility of crops and herds (see Deuteronomy 16:13-15). This would have been an especially sad time for a barren woman.

The LORD Almighty (1:3). "The LORD of hosts" in KJV and NASB. "Hosts" are armies of men or angels (the word is also used of the sun, moon, and stars). The books of Samuel emphasize that the Lord is the commander of both the armies of Israel and the armies of heaven.

LORD's House (1:9). Solomon did not build a permanent structure for the Lord's worship

For Further Study: Barrenness was a common source of grief to women in the ancient East. Read about the feelings and actions of other barren women in Genesis 16:1-16, 18:10-15, and 30:1-24. Why did God permit the barrenness in each case, and how was it overcome?

Optional Application: In prayer, Hannah showed her willingness to consecrate to the Lord something very precious to her. How does this desire affect your own prayer life?

For Thought and Discussion: At least six other children in the Bible are conceived by special acts of God: Isaac, Jacob and Esau, Samson, John the Baptist, and Jesus. What might be significant about this pattern?

For Further Study:
The book of Ruth gives a glimpse of everyday life a few decades before Samuel's birth. What can you learn in the book of Ruth about the role of women and children in Israel's history?

For Thought and Discussion: What does it mean to call God a "Rock" (see 2:2)?

For Further Study:
Compare 1 Samuel 2:1-10 with the song of Mary in Luke 1:46-55. What is similar about the causes and contents of each song? How might Hannah's song have influenced Mary's?

Optional Application: How would you describe what it means personally for you to be able to say with Hannah, "My heart rejoices in the LORD" (1 Samuel 2:1)?

until about a century later (see 1 Kings 6:1). Before this, the tabernacle—an elaborate royal tent—served as the nation's sanctuary. After Israel settled in Canaan, the tabernacle was apparently erected at Shiloh more or less permanently until the time of David. In these circumstances, it may have become "part of a larger, more permanent building complex to which the term 'temple' could legitimately be applied."[2] (Notice the mention of sleeping quarters and doors in 3:2,15.)

No razor (1:11). In dedicating her future son to the Lord, Hannah placed him under a Nazirite vow (like Samson in Judges 13:2-5). This vow was a way of expressing one's devotion or gratitude to the Lord, but it normally involved only a limited period of time rather than one's whole life (see Numbers 6:1-21; Acts 21:20-26).

Weaned (1:22). It was normal to nurse children for three years or more, since animal's milk could

---

Note how songs of praise frame the beginning and end of the books of Samuel—here in 1 Samuel 2:1-10, and in 2 Samuel 22:1-51. Together these passages express the theology of the work in song form.

---

not be refrigerated for children to drink.[3]

---

6. What are the most important truths about God that Hannah declares in her prayer in 2:1-10? What are the most important truths about mankind that she declares in this prayer?

_____

_____

_____

_____

_____

_____

7. How would you describe Hannah's character and personality as revealed in chapters 1 and 2? What were her deepest desires?

_____

_____

_____

8. Summarize the major events of Samuel's childhood as narrated in 1:21-28, 2:11, and 3:1-19.

_____

_____

_____

_____

Eli and Samuel (1 Samuel 2:12–3:21)

9. a. What are the most important facts revealed about Eli and his sons in 2:12-36? What is revealed about God in this passage?

_____

_____

_____

_____

b. To what degree might Eli have been responsible for his sons' conduct (see 2:22-25; 3:13)?

_____

_____

_____

Optional Application: In the truths that Hannah declares in her prayer in 2:1-10, what do you most want to praise God for and give Him thanks for?

For Thought and Discussion: Who do you think the author wishes to emphasize as the most important person in the opening two chapters in 1 Samuel? How does he underscore this person's significance?

Optional Application: How did Hannah demonstrate faith in entrusting her only son to be raised by a man with Eli's record as a father? How can you show similar faith in something God wants you to do?

For Thought and Discussion: What can the cases of Hannah's and Eli's sons teach us about a parent's responsibility for the spiritual nurture of children? (See also Samuel's own parenting example in 8:1-5.)

Practice of the priests (2:13). It was right to have a way to get a fair portion of fellowship offerings for the priests (see Leviticus 7:28-36), but 1 Samuel 2:15-16 shows an abuse of a fair practice. The Law specified boiled meat for the

For Thought and Discussion: On what did Samuel's success as a prophet and leader of Israel depend, according to 1 Samuel 2:19-21? How is this relevant to leaders today? How is it relevant to you?

Optional Application: How can you show yourself to be as ready as Samuel was to receive God's word?

priests (see Numbers 6:19-20). Roasting was not forbidden, but it was unreasonable for Eli's sons to refuse boiled meat (see 1 Samuel 2:15). Furthermore, the Law required that the Lord's portion be burned first before the priests got their share, but Eli's sons wanted theirs first (see 1 Samuel 2:15-16). Finally, they were threatening force (see 1 Samuel 2:16), but the gift to them was supposed to be voluntary.

10. Why do you think the story of how kingship in Israel was established begins with the birth and dedication of Samuel and the curse upon Eli's house?

_____

_____

_____

Man of God (2:27). A way of referring to a prophet.

Ancestor's family (2:27). The descendants of Aaron.

I will raise up for myself a faithful priest (2:35). "While the statement in 3:20 that Samuel was 'established' as a prophet of the Lord suggests Samuel may have been the fulfillment of this prediction, the clearer fulfillment comes in the person of Zadok, who served as high priest alongside Abiathar under David (2 Samuel 8:17) and came to later preeminence under Solomon (1 Kings 2:35)."[4]

11. In 2:27-36, how would you summarize the message of the man of God to Eli?

_____

_____

_____

_____

12. Consider the night and following morning described in 3:1-18, and summarize and outline what Eli and Samuel experienced. What is revealed about God in this passage?

_____

_____

_____

_____

For Thought and Discussion: How do you think God wanted Eli to respond to His warnings in 2:27-36 and 3:11-14?

The lamp of God (3:3). This golden lampstand stood in the Holy Place of the tabernacle. The priests were to never let the lamp go out before morning (see Leviticus 24:1-4).

---

13. How is Samuel's spiritual character and growth described in 3:1-21?

_____

_____

_____

14. Samuel "did not yet know the LORD" (3:7). To "know" someone in Hebrew signified intimate, direct relationship. After his experiences in chapter 3, in what sense did Samuel "know" the Lord in a way that he hadn't before?

_____

_____

_____

15. How does God's revelation to Samuel in 3:11-14 compare to what He had already revealed to Eli through the man of God in 2:27-36?

_____

_____

_____

For Further Study:
Samuel was "attested as a prophet of the LORD" (1 Samuel 3:20). How is the prophet Samuel associated with Moses in Psalm 99:6 and Jeremiah 15:1?

For Thought and Discussion: Samuel's name sounds like the Hebrew for "heard of God." How is this relevant to Samuel's ministry in Israel?

From Dan to Beersheba (3:20). A way of referring to the whole land of Israel and its people. Dan was in the far north and Beersheba in the far south.

16. What is most significant in the statements made about Samuel in 3:19-21?

_____

_____

Samuel was attested as a prophet of the LORD (3:20). Samuel the prophet became "the person God used to establish kingship in Israel. Samuel not only anointed both Saul and David, Israel's first two kings, but he also gave definition to the new order of God's rule over Israel that began with the incorporation of kingship into its structure. Samuel's importance as God's representative in this period of Israel's history is close to that of Moses (see Psalm 99:6; Jeremiah 15:1) since he, more than any other person, provided for covenant continuity in the transition from the rule of the judges to that of the monarchy."[5]

The Ark — Captured, Then Returned

(1 Samuel 4–6)

17. a. In 1 Samuel 4:1-11, what made it possible for the Philistines to capture the ark of God, and how did they do it?

_____

_____

_____

b. What explanation can be found in Deuteronomy 28:15,25 for Israel's defeat by the Philistines in 4:2?

26

_____

_____

_____

_____

Philistines (4:1). These traditional enemies of Israel are thought to have settled on the southern coastal plain of the Promised Land between 1500 and 1200 BC. Their five major cities (Ashdod, Gaza, Gath, Ashkelon, and Ekron) formed a strong political-military coalition. They were also technologically superior to Israel (see 1 Samuel 13:19-22). Their political, military, and technological strength made them a continuing threat to the Hebrew tribes.

The ark of the LORD's covenant (4:3). A box or chest, on the top of which were the figures of two angels (see Exodus 25:10-22). The ark contained the stone tablets on which the Ten Commandments were inscribed, along with certain other objects from the time of Israel's wilderness wanderings. It was considered the most sacred of all of the tabernacle's furnishings and symbolized God's presence in the midst of His people. The use of the ark in the overthrow of Jericho (see Joshua 6:2-21) may have encouraged Israel to try to employ it against the Philistines. The Israelites' decision to carry the ark into battle reflected a pagan belief that a god was identified with the symbol of his presence, and that his help could automatically be secured by manipulating his symbol.[6]

18. a. How did the Philistines react to the news that the ark was coming into battle (see 4:5-9)?

_____

_____

_____

For Thought and Discussion: Israel often experienced military defeats in times of spiritual decay. In the Christian life, what is the correlation between our unfaithfulness to God and the experience of hardships in life? What has been your experience in this?

For Further Study: Observe how God's glory departs from Israel in Ezekiel 10:3–11:25 and the reasons mentioned there. How does the situation in Ezekiel compare to that in 1 Samuel 4?

For Thought and Discussion: From the initial perspective of the Philistines, what was proved by their capture of the ark? But from God's perspective, what was demonstrated by the ark's capture?

b. What did they apparently know about the God of Israel? How do you think their victory over Israel affected their opinion about the Lord?

_____

_____

_____

19. In 4:12-18, how did Eli's death come about?

_____

_____

_____

20. In the description in 4:19-22, what is the significance of Eli's daughter-in-law's experience?

_____

_____

_____

_____

21. From chapters 5 and 6, summarize what happened in the Philistines' experience with the ark of God and the circumstances of how they sent it back to Israel.

_____

_____

_____

_____

22. What parallels do you see between the events involving the ark while it was among the Philistines (in chapter 5) and those that occurred when it was being returned to Israel (see 6:19–7:1)?

_____

_____

_____

_____

For Thought and Discussion: What kind of attitude on the part of the Philistines toward the God of Israel is suggested in chapters 4–6?

Dagon (5:2). Probably the grain god and principle deity of the middle Euphrates region (upriver from Babylon). Dagon's worship spread to Canaan, and he became the chief god of the Philistines (see Judges 16:21,23,26; 1 Chronicles 10:10). In Canaanite mythology, Dagon was the son (or brother) of El and the father of Baal.[7]

To this day (5:5). The time when 1 and 2 Samuel were written.

_____

For Further Study: Reflect on Samuel's call to the people (in 7:3) to return to the Lord with all their hearts. How does this compare with what you see in these passages: Deuteronomy 6:4-5; 11:1,13,22; 19:9; 30:6,16,20; Joshua 22:5; 23:11?

23. How could the Philistines tell that the ark's return to Israel was sovereignly directed by the Lord (see 6:1-12)?

_____

_____

_____

For Thought and Discussion: The books of 1 and 2 Samuel stress the importance of the chosen leader in the lives of God's people. In what ways do you see this emphasis in the rest of Scripture?

Beth Shemesh (6:9,12-13). A town of Judah near the Philistine border.

_____

24. From all that happened in relation to the ark both in Philistia and in Israel, what new understanding would the people have gained of what the ark represented?

_____

_____

_____

"A key theme of the ark narratives (1 Samuel 4–7) is that God refuses to be manipulated. Carrying the ark into battle

For Thought and Discussion: From a biblical perspective, what are the most important factors in having a correct attitude toward human leaders, both political and religious?

does not guarantee an Israelite victory (see 4:3-11), placing the ark in a Philistine temple does not ensure divine blessing (see 5:1–6:12), and looking into the ark brings death (see 6:19; see also 2 Samuel 6:6-7)."[8]

Samuel's Leadership (1 Samuel 7)

25. In your own words, how would you describe the spiritual state of Israel as indicated in 7:2 and the reasons for it?

_____

_____

_____

_____

Baals and Ashtoreths (7:4). Baal and Ashtoreth were the most important male and female Canaanite gods. The word *baal* literally meant "lord," "master," "owner," or "husband," but the term came to be applied to the deity who supposedly presided over thunder and rain, and so determined the fertility of the soil. Ashtoreth (also called Ashtaroth, Astarte, and Ishtar), was the goddess of war, love, and fertility. The worship of both Baal and Ashtoreth included immoral practices such as ritual sex and other magical rites to attain fertility. The Lord's prophets spared no effort to combat worship of these idols. (See, for example, the battle over rain and fire power in 1 Kings 17:1–18:46.) The plural terms "Baals and Ashtoreths" probably referred to the stone pillars and wooden poles used to represent the deities in their shrines.

Mizpah (7:5). A town in Benjamin, about 7.5 miles north of Jerusalem.

26. In 7:6, how did the Israelites show their determination to seek the Lord only?

_____

_____

_____

27. How would you compare the Israelites' attitude in 7:7-8 with their earlier words in 4:3?

_____

_____

_____

_____

For Thought and Discussion: What lessons for our lives today can we draw from the fact that the Lord sometimes miraculously intervenes on behalf of His people (as in 7:7-11)?

Optional Application: Look again at what the people urged Samuel to do in 7:8. In what situations in your life is this something you need to do, on behalf of others or for your own sake?

For Thought and Discussion: What do chapters 5–7 suggest about the extent to which God's honor depends on the obedience of His people?

Drew water and poured it out before the LORD (7:6). The meaning of this ceremony is uncertain. In 2 Samuel 23:13-17, it seemed for David to be an offering to the Lord as well as a symbol of the blood of men who had risked their lives to do him a kindness. Here in 7:6, the Israelites may have been expressing sorrow, humility, and repentance for their desperate condition (compare 1 Samuel 1:15; Psalm 62:8; Lamentations 2:19).

Leader (7:6). Traditionally, "judge." This was Israel's highest political office after the time of Joshua and before the inauguration of the monarchy. A judge had judicial and military authority over whole tribes or even the entire nation. Unlike kingship, the office of judge was not hereditary. Rather, each judge was chosen and empowered by God. However, their divine appointment did not normally make them priests or give them the right to serve as spiritual leaders or as mediators between God and His people. Samuel exercised religious as well as judicial authority for these reasons: His mother had consecrated him to God's service; he was probably of a priestly family; he grew up with Eli the priest; and he was gifted as a prophet as well as a judge.

28. How did God convince Israel to accept and appreciate Samuel's leadership (7:7-17)? What do you think the Lord's actions in verse 10 were meant to teach Israel?

_____

_____

_____

_____

Lesson Overview

29. What would you select as the key verse or passage in 1 Samuel 1–7 — one that best captures or reflects the dynamics of what these chapters are all about?

_____

_____

_____

_____

30. List any lingering questions you have about 1 Samuel 1–7.

_____

_____

_____

For the Group

In your first meeting, it may be helpful to turn to the front of this book and review together the "How to Use This Guide" section.

You may want to focus part of your discussion for lesson 1 on the following overall key themes from 1 Samuel. How do you see these themes developing in chapters 1–7? And what other recurring themes have you noticed?

- Divine providence—God's sovereign oversight of human and national destiny
- The destructive effects of sin
- Obedience to God
- The kingdom of God
- Leadership
- Defining success and failure

The following numbered questions in lesson 1 may stimulate your best and most helpful discussion: 2, 3, 4, 5, 6, 7, 24, 25, 28, 29, and 30.

Look also at the questions in the margin under the heading "For Thought and Discussion."

1. *NIV Study Bible* (Grand Rapids, MI: Zondervan, 1985), on 1 Samuel 1:1.
2. *NIV Study Bible*, on 1 Samuel 1:9.
3. *NIV Study Bible*, on 1 Samuel 1:22.
4. *New Geneva Study Bible* (Nashville: Thomas Nelson, 1995), on 1 Samuel 2:35.
5. *NIV Study Bible*, introduction to 1 Samuel: "Title."
6. *NIV Study Bible*, on 1 Samuel 4:3.
7. Geoffrey Bromiley, ed., *The International Standard Bible Encyclopedia*, vol. 1 (Grand Rapids, MI: Eerdmans, 1979), s.v. "Dagon"; *NIV Study Bible*, on 1 Samuel 5:2.
8. Ronald F. Youngblood, *Expositor's Bible Commentary*, ed. Frank E. Gaebelein, vol. 3, *1–2 Samuel* (Grand Rapids, MI: Zondervan, 1992), 561.

1 SAMUEL 8–15
Saul's Rise

Wanting — and Getting — a King

(1 Samuel 8–10)

1. Chapter 8 reveals differing attitudes toward establishing a monarch in Israel. From what you see in this chapter, summarize the perspectives on this issue on the part of . . .

the people of Israel:

_____

_____

_____

Samuel:

_____

_____

_____

the Lord:

_____

_____

_____

For Further Study:
Recall God's words to Samuel: "They have rejected me as their king" (1 Samuel 8:7). How is the weight of that statement from God reinforced by each of these passages — Numbers 23:21; Psalm 5:2; 47:2; 95:3; Jeremiah 10:10; Daniel 4:37; Zechariah 14:9; Malachi 1:14?

Now appoint a king to lead us, such as all the other nations have (8:5). "The institution of the monarchy was a new stage in the political and religious history of Israel, although the idea of kingship itself would have been known to Israel from the practice of its neighbors (see Judges 3:12; 4:2; 8:5). What is remarkable is not that Israel eventually installed a king, but that it resisted doing so for so long."[1]

"Their desire for a king (1 Samuel 8:5) was not in itself inappropriate, despite Samuel's initial displeasure (verse 6). Nor were they necessarily wrong in wanting a king like 'all the other nations' had (verses 5, 20). Their sin consisted in the fact that they were asking for a king 'to lead us and to go out before us and fight our battles' (verse 20). In other words, they refused to believe that the Lord would grant them victory in his own time and according to his own good pleasure (contrast 2 Samuel 8:6, 14). They were willing to exchange humble faith in the protection and power of 'the LORD Almighty' (1 Samuel 1:3) for misguided reliance on the naked strength of 'the fighting men of Israel' (2 Samuel 24:4)."[2]

2. a. What reasons did the elders of Israel give for wanting a king (see 8:1-5)?

_____

_____

_____

_____

b. What deeper reason is demonstrated in 8:20? How does Deuteronomy 7:6-11 relate to their expressed desire in 8:20?

_____

_____

_____

3. a. In 8:7-9 and 8:21-22, what did God command Samuel to do about the request for a king?

_____

_____

_____

b. In his response to Israel in 8:11-18, what does Samuel try to explain? How successful was Samuel in getting his warning through to Israel, as indicated in 1 Samuel 8:19-22?

_____

_____

_____

_____

Optional Application: Consider how Samuel responded in 8:6 when the people made a request that displeased him. On what kinds of occasions in your own life is this an example for you to follow?

For Thought and Discussion: Instead of demanding a king (as they do in chapter 8), what request could Israel have made that would have been more pleasing to the Lord?

Optional Application: What does it mean personally for you to treat God as your King?

What the king . . . will claim as his rights (8:11). "Using a description of the policies of contemporary Canaanite kings [see 8:11-17], Samuel warns the people of the burdens associated with the type of kingship they long for."[3]

Tenth (8:15). This was the customary king's tax. The Lord demanded a tenth of each family's income as His royal portion (see Leviticus 27:30-33; Numbers 18:26; Deuteronomy 14:22-29). Lands, crops, animals, and people belonged to the Lord, Israel's Great King.

No! . . . We want a king over us (8:19). "What Samuel had warned about (see 1 Samuel 8:10-18) the people continued to lust after (see verses 19-20)."[4]

For Further Study:
In Deuteronomy 17:14-20, notice the regulations concerning kingship that had long before been given to Israel through Moses, centuries before the events described in 1 Samuel 8. In that passage from Deuteronomy, (a) what were the most important stipulations regarding the selection of a king, (b) what does the passage emphasize that a king must *not* do, and (c) what does it say a king *should* do, and for what reasons?

For Further Study:
From earlier books in Scripture, we can foresee that a monarchy is coming to God's people. Look up Genesis 17:6,16 (God's promises to Abraham), Genesis 35:11 (His promise to Jacob), Genesis 49:10 (Jacob's prophetic blessing upon his son Judah), and Numbers 24:7 and 24:17-19 (oracles given by God through the pagan prophet Balaam). How do those passages indicate that God would one day give Israel a human king?

4. Summarize the events in chapter 9 leading up to Saul's encounter with Samuel.

_____

_____

_____

_____

_____

Prophet (9:9). The Hebrew word for "prophet" comes from the verb "to call." In 1 Samuel 3, Isaiah 6, and Jeremiah 1, we learn more of why prophets were named "called ones."

Seer (9:9). Along with the general term "man of God," the word "seer" was an older way of referring to a prophet. The Hebrew word is a participle of the verb "to see," but it does not indicate that visions or dreams were always the way God spoke to the prophet. Just as in English, "see" was used metaphorically to mean "perceive" or "understand."[5] God apparently revealed His will to Samuel verbally rather than visually (see 3:2-14; 8:6-9,21-22; 9:15-17; 15:10-11; 16:1-2,6-12).

High place (9:12). The Canaanite custom was to build altars on hills. Thus when the Israelites entered Canaan, they found pagan places of worship and sacrifice scattered throughout the land on higher elevations. At the time of 9:12, Israel's central sanctuary was not in use because the ark was separated from the tabernacle. Shiloh had been destroyed, and Eli's priestly family was decimated. So Samuel was apparently performing sacrifices at local altars around the country. Samuel's action presumably did not involve pagan practices, but later the Israelites continued to use those high places for Canaanite-style worship after the temple was built in Jerusalem. The use of sites long associated with Canaanite worship became a source of contamination for Israel, so the prophets eventually condemned this practice (see 1 Kings 3:2; 2 Kings 17:7-18; 21:2-9; 23:4-25).

Anoint (9:16). Consecrating a person as priest (see Exodus 29:7), prophet (see 1 Kings 19:16), or king (see 1 Samuel 10:1) involved pouring spiced olive oil on his head. Oil seems to have symbolized favor, blessing, and prosperity, and anointing signified separation to the Lord for a particular task as well as divine equipping for that task.[6] While prophets and priests were anointed, the term "anointed one" was usually reserved for kings (but see Zechariah 4:14). The Hebrew term is *meshiach*, from which we get "Messiah" and the Greek translation, "Christ."

Thigh (9:24). This piece was normally reserved for consecrated priests (see Leviticus 7:32-33).

---

5. What impressions do you get of Saul's character from 9:2-21? How would you evaluate Saul's concern in 9:7 to offer a gift to the man of God?

_____

_____

_____

_____

6. What signs of God's sovereignty and compassion over the great and small affairs of life do you find in chapters 9 and 10?

_____

_____

_____

_____

For Further Study: In Judges 8:22-23 and 9:1-57, what warnings were given concerning the dangers of monarchy?

For Further Study: In what ways do you see Samuel's warnings in 1 Samuel 8:10-18 being fulfilled in 1 Kings 12:1-15?

For Thought and Discussion: Sometimes desires we have that are legitimate in themselves (like the desire of the Israelites for a king) may become harmful and wrong because of other influencing factors. What can help us discern when this is happening to us?

For Further Study: Compare Saul's desire to give a gift to the prophet (in 9:7) with what you see in 1 Kings 14:3 and 22:6,8,18 and 2 Kings 4:42 and 5:15-16. How did paying prophets ultimately affect their performance?

39

7. What evidence do you see in chapters 9 and 10 that Saul's elevation to the throne was *not* the result of his personal ambition?

_____

_____

_____

_____

"The offices of king and prophet arose simultaneously in Israel. Saul, the first king (see 1 Samuel 10:24), was anointed by Samuel, who stands at the head of the prophetic line (see 9:6-10, 19; Acts 3:24; 13:20; Hebrews 11:32) as promised to Moses (see Deuteronomy 18:15-18). If the task of the king was to administer the covenant, that of the prophet was to interpret its demands. In matters relative to God's will as revealed through his word, the submission of kings to prophets was self-understood (see 1 Samuel 13:13; 15:22-23; 2 Samuel 12:7-14)."[7]

Procession of prophets (10:5,10). "Small communities of men . . . banded together in spiritually decadent times for mutual cultivation of their religious zeal."[8] They were called the "company of the prophets" (see 1 Kings 20:35; 2 Kings 2:3-15; 4:1,38; 5:22; 6:1; 9:1). Prophets such as Samuel and Elijah were often mentors to the prophetic communities.

Is Saul also among the prophets? (10:11). The observers may have known enough about Saul to be astonished to find him among men passionately devoted to God. Or the questions may be insults to prophets ("What was he [Saul], a respectable local citizen, doing in the presence

40

of these roaming madmen of unknown and dubious antecedents?"[9]).

Who is their father? (10:12). Perhaps a gibe about Samuel, the prophets' spiritual father. Or it may be a recognition that God is the Father of prophetic inspiration and can give it to anyone, even Saul.[10]

Benjamin was taken by lot (10:20). The high priest wore an outer garment called an ephod (see 2:28; 14:3), in which he carried the Urim and Thummin, which seem to have been small stones or lots that were cast like dice to gain yes-or-no answers from the Lord (see 14:36-37,41-42; 22:10; 23:1-4,6,9-12). The assumption was that God would sovereignly control how they fell so as to reveal the correct answer (see Proverbs 16:33).

Rights and duties of kingship (10:25). Probably the laws relating to and limiting the authority of Israel's king (see Deuteronomy 17:14-20). God may have revealed further guidelines through Samuel to show clearly how Israel's king must be different from pagan kings and how the monarchy would not conflict with the Lord's status as Great King.

For Thought and Discussion: What did the "scoundrels" expect of a king (see 10:27)? Was this a godly expectation? Why or why not?

For Thought and Discussion: To what extent do these first chapters of 1 Samuel reflect progress in Israel's history?

8. In 10:2-10, why do you think Samuel prophesied to Saul these specific events that were about to happen to him?

_____

_____

_____

9. From what you see in 10:6-7 and 10:9-12, how was Saul divinely prepared—as well as divinely chosen—to lead his nation?

_____

_____

41

_____

_____

Saul's Early Reign (1 Samuel 11–14)

10. In what ways is Saul more firmly established as king by the events recorded in chapter 11?

_____

_____

_____

11. In 11:1-6, what prompted Saul's first public action?

_____

_____

_____

Ammonite (11:1). The Ammonites were descended from Lot, Abraham's nephew, by an incestuous union (see Genesis 19:31-38). They were thus distantly related to Israel. The territory they occupied was northeast of the Dead Sea, across the Jordan River from Israel. Seeing Israel hard pressed by the Philistines on the west, the Ammonites seized the chance to move against Israel on the east.

Make a treaty with us (11:1). The inhabitants of Jabesh Gilead tried to buy Nahash off. The term translated "treaty" is rendered elsewhere as "covenant," especially when used of Israel's relationship to God. God had forbidden Israel to make any such treaties with the people of Canaan (see Exodus 34:12-16; Deuteronomy 7:2). The Jabeshites would have been willing to serve, but God was working for their salvation.

Gouge out (11:2). "Besides causing humiliation . . . the loss of the right eye would destroy the military capability of the archers."[11]

Messengers throughout Israel (11:3). Nahash apparently felt so convinced of his military superiority, even over all Israel, that he consented to this unusual request. Israel's leader, Samuel, was elderly, and Israel's tribes were only a loose confederacy at this time. (In fact, it was just this lack of a strong central authority that had influenced the people to demand a king in the first place; see 8:5,20.) The messengers from Jabesh Gilead had to contact the elders of the various tribes individually, a complicated and time-consuming task.

12. a. In 11:3-11, summarize the chain of events that led to the rescue of Jabesh Gilead. What was Saul's role in all of this?

_____

_____

_____

_____

b. Why did this event convince all Israel that Saul was the Lord's choice to be king (see 11:6-12)?

_____

_____

_____

For Thought and Discussion: Since Nahash rejected the Jabeshites' offer of submission, what seems to have been his objective in attacking this city (see 11:1-2)?

For Further Study: Gilgal was where Saul's kingship was reaffirmed (see 1 Samuel 11:14-15). What significance does this place have in Israel's history, according to the following passages: Joshua 4:19; 5:1-10; 9:6; 10:6,43; 14:6; Judges 2:1?

Optional Application: For believers today, what possible application might 1 Samuel 11 have to our daily spiritual warfare?

The Spirit of God came powerfully upon him (11:6). This phrase occurs often in the Old Testament (see Numbers 24:2; Judges 3:10; 6:34; 11:29; 13:25; 14:6,19; 15:14; 1 Samuel 16:13; 1 Chronicles 12:18; 2 Chronicles 15:1; 20:14; 24:20). It normally speaks of a special empowerment granted to someone by God to accomplish a particular task. It is never used for a conversion experience in the New Testament sense. Nor does it imply that everything the individual does is according to God's will (Judges 11:29-31 is an example). Israel's judges were usually marked out in this way.

Optional Application:
Chapters 11–12 show us two men committed to serving God's people. What has God called you to do in serving others in the body of Christ with the same commitment? What might it cost you at this time to carry out this calling, and are you willing to pay that cost?

Optional Application:
Samuel's life was a model of integrity. To what degree are you able to stand up and say the kinds of things that Samuel said in 12:3-5? Reflect on the degree of integrity in your own standards and behavior. Are there any habits or choices you need to change?

If both you and the king . . . follow the LORD your God (12:14). "When God allowed the people of Israel to have a human king, he gave them a king only as God's earthly vice-regent or deputy, who is responsible to the Lord for his actions and subject to his commands."[12] (See also 2 Samuel 12:9.)

13. Summarize the main points in each part of Samuel's farewell address to the nation.

12:1-5

_____

_____

_____

12:6-13

_____

_____

_____

12:14-18

_____

_____

_____

12:19-25

_____

_____

_____

Testify against me (12:3). As Samuel passed the leadership to Saul, he demanded that Israel compare his performance to the moral guidelines laid down by God's Law.

Thunder and rain (12:17-18). In Palestine, rainy seasons come in the late fall and early spring. The wheat harvest takes place in early summer, a time when rain is rare. Samuel's ability to call upon the Lord to send rain was a miracle that validated his words. Also, it demonstrated that the Lord was the true ruler of the rains and alone merited Israel's worship and trust.

For Thought and Discussion: In 12:23, notice how Samuel viewed his obligations toward God's people as a prophet. Among God's people today, who bears that same responsibility, and in what way?

14. As Saul is confirmed as king, how was the Lord's supreme kingship also reaffirmed, according to what you see in these passages?

    11:13

    _____

    _____

    12:7-15

    _____

    _____

    12:20-25

    _____

    _____

For Thought and Discussion: Why would it be a sin for Samuel to cease to pray for Israel (see 12:23)?

Optional Application: With 12:23 in mind, would it be a sin for you to cease to pray for someone?

15. Review 12:12-25. In Israel's transition to monarchy, what changes had taken place? What things had not changed?

    _____

    _____

    _____

    _____

For Further Study: Compare Samuel's farewell address in 1 Samuel 12 with the apostle Paul's words to the Ephesian elders in Acts 20:17-35. What similarities do you see?

For Thought and Discussion: According to 12:1-25, why does trusting in a king — without obeying the Lord — result only in a false security?

16. Observe the words Samuel used in 12:14 to describe how Israel should treat the Lord: "fear . . . serve . . . obey . . . do not rebel . . . follow" (also compare 12:24). How would you describe in your own words the actions and attitudes Samuel was urging?

For Thought and Discussion: What do you learn from 13:5-7 about the balance of power between Israel and the Philistines?

17. What are the most important things revealed about Saul in the events recorded in chapters 13 and 14?

_____

_____

_____

_____

Reigned over Israel forty-two years (13:1). The Hebrew text here for the length of Saul's reign is not clear. Paul implied that it lasted forty years (see Acts 13:21). If Saul was thirty in chapter 11, then quite a few years have passed by the time indicated in chapter 13. Saul's oldest son has had time to grow up and become a commander of one of Saul's armies.

18. a. According to Saul (in 13:11-12), what prompted him to offer the sacrifice, rather than wait for Samuel as instructed?

_____

_____

_____

b. What do you see as the full significance of the words spoken to Saul by Samuel in 13:13-14?

_____

_____

_____

Foolish thing (13:13). The Hebrew term for fool meant someone morally as well as intellectually deficient (compare 1 Samuel 25:25; 26:21; 2 Samuel 24:10).

A man after his own heart (13:14). This is the first indication that Saul was unqualified at the deepest level for his position. Though he had been divinely appointed and confirmed by the people, he was not above replacement (compare 2:30). While Saul's heart had been changed by God (see 10:9), he did not necessarily experience conversion in the New Testament sense or a complete spiritual transformation.

For Further Study: God sought "a man after his own heart" to serve as Israel's king (13:14). Why is this heart dynamic so important, according to what you see in these passages: Exodus 25:2; Deuteronomy 4:29; 5:29; 6:5-6; 8:5; 10:12,16; 11:13,18; Joshua 22:5; 24:23; 1 Samuel 2:1; 7:3?

"Yahweh's promise of the kingdom to David begins in a threat (1 Samuel 13:14)."[13]

For Thought and Discussion: What do we learn in 14:1-52 about Jonathan's character and faith?

19. After Samuel left Saul, only six hundred of the original Israelite troops stayed with the king (see 13:15). Besides an overwhelming numerical superiority, what other advantage did the Philistines possess, according to 13:16-22?

_____

_____

_____

_____

Raiding parties (13:17). "The purpose of these Philistine contingents was not to engage the Israelites in battle, but to plunder the land and demoralize its inhabitants."[14]

Not . . . a sword or spear (13:22). Without blacksmiths to work iron, the Israelites were left to fight with slingshots and bows and arrows.

20. a. What are the most important things revealed about Saul's son Jonathan in chapter 14?

47

Optional Application: For believers today, what possible application might 1 Samuel 13–14 have to our daily spiritual warfare?

For Further Study: In the book of Esther, read how one of Saul's descendants received a chance to make amends for Saul's failure to kill Agag, the Amalekite king (see Esther 2:5; 3:1).

b. How would you summarize the role played by Jonathan in the conflict described in 13:23–14:23?

_____

_____

_____

21. How did God enable Israel to gain the upper hand against Philistia on this occasion, according to 14:15,20?

_____

_____

_____

_____

Wearing an ephod (14:3). The term was used for various garments. The ephod worn by the high priest was a "sleeveless garment . . . to which two shoulder pieces were attached and around which fitted a belt. To the shoulder pieces were affixed two onyx stones engraved with the names of the twelve tribes. . . . At the front of the garment . . . hung the breastpiece of twelve precious stones symbolizing the twelve tribes."[15] Another kind of ephod was worn by priests, by Samuel, by David, and perhaps by others (see 1 Samuel 2:18; 22:18; 2 Samuel 6:14). Some scholars think it was a kind of loincloth.[16] Others describe it as "a close-fitting, sleeveless pullover, usually of hip length" worn over one's robe or tunic.[17]

Saul built an altar (14:35). The Israelite troops were so hungry they were slaughtering the Philistines' livestock and eating it without making sure the blood had been drained. This violated the Law's prohibition against eating blood (see Leviticus 17:10-14; 19:26; Deuteronomy 12:16). To prevent this breach of the Law, Saul hastily erected an altar to ensure that all the animals were properly butchered.

Saul's Rejection (1 Samuel 15)

"In [chapter 13] obedience was the stone on which Saul stumbled; here it is the rock that crushes him."[18]

22. Briefly summarize what happens at each stage of the conflict that's described in chapter 15.

_____

_____

_____

_____

Amalekites . . . Kenites (15:3,6). The Amalekites were descended from Esau (see Genesis 36:12-16) and occupied the territory south of Israel known as the Negev. Though related to Israel, they appear in the Old Testament only as enemies of God. They were the first to attack the Hebrews after their liberation from Egypt (see Exodus 17:8-13). Later, after Israel's refusal to enter the Promised Land, the Amalekites defeated them (see Numbers 14:41-45), and during the period of the judges they repeatedly harassed Israel (see Judges 3:13; 6:3-40). The Kenites, on the other hand, were unrelated to Israel but had a generally good relationship with Israel from the Exodus onward (see Numbers 10:29; Judges 1:16). That is why Saul sought to spare them when he went against the Amalekites.

For Further Study: Compare 1 Samuel 15 to Joshua 7.

For Further Study: Review what is indicated about God in 15:11, 15:29, and 15:35. How do these truths compare with what you see in the following passages: Genesis 6:5-7; Exodus 32:12-14; Numbers 23:19; Deuteronomy 32:36; Judges 2:18; 2 Samuel 24:16; Psalm 90:13; 106:45; 110:4; 135:14?

Optional Application: What clear and direct orders has the Lord given you? How completely are you obeying Him?

Optional Application: Fear twice moved Saul to disobey God (see 13:11-12; 15:24). Has fear recently led you to disobey Him? In this season of your life, what tempts you most strongly to disobey God? And how can you overcome this temptation?

Optional Application: Pride contributed to Saul's disobedience. In what ways is pride a problem in any area of your life? Ask God to help you learn true, selfless humility.

For Thought and Discussion: How does the prophet Samuel model courage, compassion, and sternness in his response to Saul in 13:13-15 and 15:13-35?

For Thought and Discussion: What similarities and differences do you see between the judgment upon Saul and that upon Eli at the beginning of this book?

23. a. What are the most important instructions that Samuel gives to Saul in 15:1-3?

_____

_____

_____

b. How closely did Saul's actions conform to the command he had received through Samuel in 15:1-3? (See also verses 15 and 20-21.)

_____

_____

_____

Totally destroy (15:3). God had commanded Israel to utterly destroy the Canaanite tribes because their sinful religious practices threatened to corrupt His people (see Deuteronomy 7:1-5, 17-26). This destruction involved all the people belonging to the group in question but not always all their possessions (see Joshua 6:17-21; 8:1-2). The divine command to destroy the Amalekites seems to have been motivated less by a concern for Israel's purity than by a decision to judge them for what they had done to Israel previously. God may also have been once more testing Saul's obedience.

24. What did God say to Samuel about Saul's performance (see 15:10-11)? What is revealed about God and His character in these verses? What is revealed about Samuel in these verses? What is revealed about Saul in verse 12?

_____

_____

_____

25. In the conversation recorded in 15:13-30, what are the most revealing statements made by Saul? What are the most important statements

made by Samuel? What do Samuel's words reveal and emphasize regarding the character of God?

_____

_____

_____

26. Summarize in a sentence or two the declaration of Samuel in 15:22-23. How did this declaration affect Saul? (Compare 15:20-21 with 15:24-25.)

_____

_____

_____

_____

27. From 15:31-35, summarize the events that follow Samuel's encounter with Saul. What is revealed here about God, and what do you see as the significance of it?

_____

_____

_____

_____

For Thought and Discussion: What does 15:22-35 imply about Samuel's personality and the depth of his relationship with the Lord?

For Thought and Discussion: How would you evaluate the harshness of God's judgment upon Saul, as stated by Samuel in 1 Samuel 15:28?

For Further Study: How does God's judgment upon Saul (in 1 Samuel 15:28) compare with His judgment upon Moses in Numbers 20:10-12?

For Thought and Discussion: Keeping in mind God's judgment on Saul (in 15:28), what judgment from Him are Christians subject to in this life for disobedience?

"Saul's failure brought about not a new dispensation but a different king, a man 'better than' him (15:28), a man after God's own heart (see 13:14)."[19]

Lesson Overview

"The book of 1 Samuel establishes the principle that the king in Israel is to be subject to the word of God as conveyed through his prophets. In other words, obedience to the word of God is the necessary condition for a king to be acceptable to the God of Israel. This is what Jesus the Messiah-King did in his life of obedience to God the Father, even up to 'death on a cross' (Philippians 2:8)."[20]

28. What would you select as the key verse or passage in 1 Samuel 8–15 — one that best captures or reflects the dynamics of what these chapters are all about?

_____

_____

_____

_____

29. List any lingering questions you have about 1 Samuel 8–15.

_____

_____

_____

_____

For the Group

You may want to focus part of your discussion for lesson 2 on the following overall key themes from 1 Samuel. How do you see these themes developing in chapters 8–15? What additional recurring themes do you notice?

• Divine providence — God's sovereign oversight of human and national destiny
• The destructive effects of sin
• Obedience to God

- The kingdom of God
- Leadership
- Defining success and failure

The following numbered questions in lesson 2 may stimulate your best and most helpful discussion: 5, 10, 15, 17, 18, 20, 24, 25, 26, 28, and 29.

Look also at the questions in the margin under the heading "For Thought and Discussion."

1. *New Geneva Study Bible* (Nashville: Thomas Nelson, 1995), introduction to 1 Samuel: "Date and Occasion."
2. Ronald F. Youngblood, *Expositor's Bible Commentary*, ed. Frank E. Gaebelein, vol. 3, *1–2 Samuel* (Grand Rapids, MI: Zondervan, 1992), 558.
3. *NIV Study Bible* (Grand Rapids, MI: Zondervan, 1985), on 1 Samuel 8:11.
4. Youngblood, 562.
5. G. V. Smith, "Prophet, Prophecy," in *The International Standard Bible Encyclopedia*, vol. 3 (Grand Rapids, MI: Eerdmans, 1979), 987.
6. *NIV Study Bible*, on 1 Samuel 9:16.
7. Youngblood, 561.
8. *NIV Study Bible*, on 1 Samuel 10:5.
9. D. F. Payne, "1 Samuel," in *The New Bible Commentary: Revised*, ed. Donald Guthrie, et al. (Grand Rapids, MI: Eerdmans, 1970), 292.
10. *NIV Study Bible*, on 1 Samuel 10:12.
11. *NIV Study Bible*, on 1 Samuel 11:2.
12. *ESV Study Bible* (Wheaton, IL: Crossway, 2008), introduction to 1–2 Samuel: "1 Samuel Key Themes."
13. Dale Ralph Davis, *2 Samuel: Out of Every Adversity*, Focus on the Bible Commentary Series (Fearn, Scotland: Christian Focus, 1999), 60–61.
14. *NIV Study Bible*, on 1 Samuel 13:17.
15. Allen C. Myers, ed., *The Eerdmans Bible Dictionary* (Grand Rapids, MI: Eerdmans, 1987), s.v. "ephod."
16. C. de Wit, "Dress," in *The New Bible Dictionary*, 2nd ed., ed. J. D. Douglas (Leicester, England: InterVarsity, 1982), 291.
17. *NIV Study Bible*, on 1 Samuel 14:3.
18. Robert P. Gordon, *1 and 2 Samuel* (Exeter, England: Paternoster, 1986), 142.
19. Youngblood, 562.
20. *ESV Study Bible*, introduction to 1–2 Samuel: "Purpose, Occasion, and Background."

1 SAMUEL 16–18

David's Rise

"The story of the rise of David in the second half of 1 Samuel prepares for the full-scale kingship of David in 2 Samuel."[1]

David's Anointing (1 Samuel 16)

"Yahweh's promise of the kingdom to David . . . becomes visible — at least to Samuel — in the anointing among Jesse's family (1 Samuel 16:1-13)."[2]

1. Samuel's mission in 16:1-13 is to anoint a new king. How would you put into your own words what God said to Samuel in 16:7? Explain what happened when Samuel anointed David (see 16:13).

_____

_____

_____

_____

2. Notice the multiple ways that David is described in 16:18. Think about the relative importance of each element in that description. List them here in their order of importance, and explain why you rate them in that order.

For Thought and Discussion: Why exactly did God choose David to be king over Israel? Do we really know for sure?

For Further Study: While the judges were raised up spontaneously by God, the kings were called or confirmed by prophets. How do you see this in these passages: 1 Samuel 10:1; 1 Kings 1:32-39; 11:29-39; 19:15-16; 2 Kings 9:1-10?

For Further Study:
The ancients felt strongly about the superiority and priority of the firstborn, but notice how the book of Genesis repeatedly stresses God's choice of a younger brother for special blessing or service — see Genesis 17:18-21; 25:23; 27:27-29,39-40; 37:5-11. What reason can you give for this? (See also Romans 9:16-21.)

Optional Application: If you are in a position of choosing someone for leadership or partnership, ask the Lord to help you to choose someone with the heart He wants, and not to be distracted by outward appearances.

Optional Application: Do you evaluate people and situations by how they appear outwardly, or do you look deeper and consider them from God's point of view? How can you cultivate the ability to see the heart, as God does?

3. As he grew older, Saul began to experience fits of depression, jealousy, and violence (see 19:9-10). What caused these psychological problems, according to 15:24-26 and 16:14?

4. As a remedy for Saul's affliction, his servants suggested a musician like David (see 16:14-18). What was it about David that impressed his contemporaries (see 16:18)?

David's Test (1 Samuel 17)

5. In chapter 17, read carefully over the account of the famous encounter between David and Goliath. From verses 17:1-32, how would you summarize the most important details leading up to David's offer to fight Goliath in verse 32?

Champion (17:4). "The ancient Greeks, to whom the Philistines were apparently related, sometimes decided issues of war through chosen champions who met in combat between the armies. Through this economy of warriors the judgment of the gods on the matter at stake was determined. . . . Israel too may have known this practice (2 Samuel 2:14-16)."[3]

---

6. We hear David speak for the first time in 17:26. How is his attitude toward the situation different from everyone else's? (See also 17:34-37.)

_____

_____

_____

7. How did Goliath's repeated challenges affect Israel's army (see 17:11,24)?

_____

_____

_____

8. In 17:28, how is David viewed by his older brother, Eliab? In 17:33, how is David viewed by Saul? In 17:42-44, how is David viewed by Goliath? In contrast, what did the Lord see in David's heart (remember what the Lord had said in 16:7)?

_____

_____

_____

_____

9. Summarize the interaction between Saul and David in 17:32-39. What are the most important things revealed in these verses about David? What are the most important things revealed here about Saul?

_____

_____

_____

For Further Study: What do the following New Testament principles teach about the principles of election or calling for special ministry: Matthew 4:18-22; Luke 9:1-5; 10:1-12; Acts 9:1-6; 13:1-3; 1 Corinthians 12:27-31; 1 Timothy 3:1-13?

For Thought and Discussion: In what ways are Christians today ever called to make a stand similar to the stand David made against Goliath in 1 Samuel 17?

Optional Application: David's deep concern for God's honor led him to challenge Goliath. How should our own concern for God's honor be manifested?

Optional Application: "The Lord . . . will rescue me," David affirmed (17:37). With that same degree of confidence, what deliverances can you affirm that God will grant to *you?*

For Thought and Discussion: What lesson do you see in the contrast in weaponry between Goliath and David (see 17:5-7,40)?

10. How would you explain the confidence in God that David articulated in 17:37?

11. Summarize the most important details in the encounter between David and Goliath in 17:40-51. What are the most important things these verses reveal about David?

Stones (17:40). "Usually the stones chosen were round and smooth and somewhat larger than a baseball. When hurled by a master slinger, they probably traveled at close to 100 miles per hour."[4]

12. What do you find most significant in David's understanding of God as revealed in his words to Goliath in 17:45-47?

13. What lesson did David say would be taught by his victory over Goliath (see 17:46-47)?

58

14. From 17:51-58, summarize the aftermath of David's fight with Goliath.

_____

_____

_____

_____

Optional Application: For believers today, what possible application might 1 Samuel 17 have to our daily spiritual warfare?

Whose son is that young man? (17:55). "The seeming contradiction between verses 55-58 and 16:14-23 may be resolved by noting that prior to this time David was not a permanent resident at Saul's court (see verse 15; 18:2), so that Saul's knowledge of David and his family may have been minimal. Further, Saul may have been so incredulous at David's courage that he was wondering if his family background and social standing might explain his extraordinary conduct."[5]

David with Saul and His Family

(1 Samuel 18)

15. Summarize the events narrated in chapter 18. What does this chapter reveal about Saul? What does it reveal about Jonathan? What does it reveal about David?

_____

_____

_____

_____

16. What significance do you see in the actions taken by Jonathan toward David in 18:3-4?

_____

_____

"Yahweh's promise of the kingdom to David . . . hangs as a suspicion over a tormented Saul (1 Samuel 18:8)."[6]

17. How is Jonathan's help for David emphasized in 18:1-4? What important principles of friendship does Jonathan exemplify?

_____

_____

_____

Covenant (18:3). This term covered treaties between nations (see 11:1), contracts between individuals, marriage vows, and pacts between friends. (The latter is the thought in 18:3.) The covenant between God and Israel had elements of a friendship pact and a marriage vow, but it was primarily a treaty between a sovereign and a subject people. The ideas of commitment, loyalty, affection, intimate personal knowledge, and mutual responsibilities run through all covenants. A covenant could be either bilateral or unilateral — created either by mutual consent or by the will of one party that the other simply accepted. The covenant between Jonathan and David was probably by mutual consent. God's covenant with Israel, however, was due exclusively to His initiative and sustained only through His grace (see Deuteronomy 5:2-3; 9:4-29; 10:12-16).

Robe . . . tunic . . . sword . . . bow . . . belt (18:4). These gifts for David from Jonathan ratified the covenant and symbolized that he was giving himself to David. The gift of his personal possessions — his clothes and weapons — implies that Jonathan was making David an honorary member of the royal family. They may also suggest that Jonathan recognized that David, not he, would succeed Saul as king (see 20:14-15).

David his tens of thousands (18:7). Hebrew poetry is structured with parallelism rather than rhyme. Since ten thousand was the customary parallel for one thousand (see Deuteronomy 32:30; Psalm 91:7; Micah 6:7), 1 Samuel 18:7 is simply a poetic way of saying "Saul and David have slain thousands." "It is a measure of Saul's insecurity and jealousy that he read [the women's] intentions incorrectly and took offense. His resentment may have been initially triggered by the mention of David's name alongside his own."[7]

---

18. Saul had favored David (see 16:21-22; 17:55–18:2), but then turned against him. What reasons for this turnaround do you see in these passages?

    18:6-9

    _____

    _____

    _____

    18:12,15,28-29

    _____

    _____

    _____

19. Describe the progression in the tactics Saul used to try to eliminate David, as evidenced in these passages:

    18:10-11

    _____

    _____

    _____

18:17

_____

_____

_____

18:20-25

_____

_____

_____

Prophesying (18:10). "The Hebrew for this word
is sometimes used to indicate uncontrolled
ecstatic behavior . . . and is best understood
in that sense in this context."[8] "Prophesying"
could also be used for praise and worship of
God under the influence of the Holy Spirit
(see Numbers 11:24-29; 1 Samuel 10:5,10-11;
19:23). In other situations, it meant the authoritative proclamation of God's word, including
comments on the present, instructions for the
future, and prediction of the future.

Older daughter (18:17). David was entitled to
marry Merab because of his triumph over
Goliath (see 17:25), but now Saul adds more
conditions.

No other price (18:25). The father of the bride
usually received a sum (see Genesis 34:12;
Exodus 22:16) "as compensation for the loss of
his daughter and insurance for her support if
widowed."[9]

20. What contrasts between Saul and David do you
observe in chapter 18? What indications are
there in chapter 18 that God was actively
watching over David?

_____

_____

_____

_____

Lesson Overview

21. How do you most clearly see God's sovereign
    control of the events in chapters 16–18?

    _____

    _____

    _____

22. Scripture emphasizes that David was a man
    after God's own heart (see 1 Samuel 13:14; Acts
    13:22). What confirmation of this do you see in
    1 Samuel 16–18? And what evidence here helps
    us understand what that description means?

    _____

    _____

    _____

    _____

23. What do these chapters reveal about David's gifts
    and abilities as a future leader of all God's people?

    _____

    _____

    _____

    _____

24. What would you select as the key verse or pas-
    sage in 1 Samuel 16–18 — one that best cap-
    tures or reflects the dynamics of what these
    chapters are all about?

    _____

    _____

    _____

25. List any lingering questions you have about
    1 Samuel 16–18.

_____

_____

_____

For the Group

You may want to focus part of your discussion for
lesson 3 on the following overall key themes from
1 Samuel. How do you see these themes developing in chapters 16–18? What additional recurring
themes do you notice?

• Divine providence—God's sovereign oversight
  of human and national destiny
• The destructive effects of sin
• Obedience to God
• The kingdom of God
• Leadership
• Defining success and failure

    The following numbered questions in lesson 3
may stimulate your best and most helpful discussion: 9, 10, 12, 17, 20, 21, 22, 23, 24, and 25.
    Remember to look also at the "For Thought and
Discussion" questions in the margin.

1. *ESV Study Bible* (Wheaton, IL: Crossway, 2008), introduction to 1–2 Samuel: "Purpose, Occasion, and Background."
2. Dale Ralph Davis, *2 Samuel: Out of Every Adversity*, Focus
   on the Bible Commentary Series (Fearn, Scotland:
   Christian Focus, 1999), 60–61.
3. *NIV Study Bible* (Grand Rapids, MI: Zondervan, 1985), on
   1 Samuel 17:4.
4. *NIV Study Bible*, on 1 Samuel 17:40.
5. *NIV Study Bible*, on 1 Samuel 17:55.
6. Davis, 60–61.
7. *NIV Study Bible*, on 1 Samuel 18:7.
8. *NIV Study Bible*, on 1 Samuel 18:10.
9. *NIV Study Bible*, on 1 Samuel 18:25.

1 SAMUEL 19–26

Escapes

David Departs (1 Samuel 19–20)

1. Describe the continuing progression in the tactics Saul used to try to eliminate David, as indicated in these passages:

19:1-7

_____

_____

_____

19:9-10

_____

_____

_____

19:11-24

_____

_____

_____

For Further Study: Compare 19:11 with the situation described in the heading or title to Psalm 59. In what ways does the content of Psalm 59 appear to reflect David's circumstances and spiritual condition in 1 Samuel 19?

Optional Application: Think about what envy did to Saul. How can you guard against this sin infecting you?

New Moon feast (20:5). On the first day of each month, the people of Israel consecrated the month to the Lord with special sacrifices, blowing trumpets, and rest from work (see Numbers 10:10; 28:11-15).

Optional Application: How easy is it for you to form committed, intimate friendships, like that between David and Jonathan? What do such relationships require of you in terms of character and lifestyle?

Optional Application: To whom can you be the kind of friend that Jonathan was to David?

2. In the conversation between Jonathan and David in 20:1-9, what is David's basic concern? What is Jonathan's perspective regarding that concern?

_____

_____

_____

Show kindness (20:8,14-15). The definitive way in which covenanted people were supposed to treat each other was with *hesed*—kindness, loving-kindness, steadfast love, mercy, loyalty. This word occurs dozens of times in the Old Testament to describe the way God treats His covenant people and the way they are supposed to treat Him and each other. David and Jonathan had a right to expect *hesed* from each other because of the covenant between them. David wanted Jonathan to show *hesed* to him by saving his life. Jonathan wanted David to do it by not wiping out his family when he became king. The first ruler of a new dynasty often murdered all the rival claimants to the throne from the preceding dynasty, and Jonathan did not want this to happen to him and his children. He was that convinced that David would be king. When the Jews translated their Scriptures into Greek in 200 BC, they chose the word *agape* ("love") most often as the Greek equivalent of *hesed*. (See the idea of *hesed*, covenant love, behind John 15:12-13.)

3. a. What are the major details in the plan Jonathan lays out in 20:10-23? What is the significance of Jonathan's request from David in 20:14-15?

_____

_____

_____

_____

66

b. What is the significance of the covenant Jonathan makes with David in 20:16-17 and 20:23? (Refer also to 18:3-4.) What special significance do you see in Jonathan's words in 20:42?

_____

_____

_____

_____

Abner (20:25). Saul's cousin and the commander of his army (see 14:50).

Son of a perverse and rebellious woman (20:30). This Hebrew idiom, like its English equivalent, was meant to characterize Jonathan, not his mother.[1]

4. Two of Saul's children—Michal and Jonathan—sought to help David when Saul turned against him. What specific help do they give David in 19:1-7 and 20:1-42?

_____

_____

_____

_____

5. What does Jonathan's attitude toward inheriting his father's throne (see 20:13-16,31-32) say about his character?

_____

_____

_____

_____

For Thought and Discussion: The Law commanded the Israelites to love their neighbors as themselves (see Leviticus 19:18; 1 Samuel 18:1; Matthew 22:34-40). How does Jonathan demonstrate what this means in his actions toward David?

For Further Study: On the theme of friendship, study Proverbs 14:20; 17:17; 18:24; 19:4,6; 22:11,24; 27:6,10. In what ways do you see David and Jonathan demonstrating these principles?

For Thought and Discussion: What do you think David is learning through the difficulties he is suffering because of Saul's opposition?

For Further Study:
Compare 21:10-11 with the situation described in the heading to Psalm 56. In what ways does the content of Psalm 56 appear to reflect David's circumstances and spiritual condition in 1 Samuel 21?

For Further Study:
The Law required that only priests could eat the bread of the Presence (see Leviticus 24:9). What lesson did Jesus draw from the fact that Ahimelek gave this holy bread to David in 1 Samuel 21? (See Matthew 12:1-8, especially verses 3-4,7.)

Optional Application: What lessons for your life can you draw from David's example during this season when he was a fugitive?

For Further Study:
Compare 21:12–22:1 with the situation described in the heading to Psalm 34. In what ways does the content of Psalm 34 appear to reflect David's circumstances and spiritual condition in 1 Samuel 21 and 22?

6. What important principles of friendship does Jonathan exemplify in 19:1-7 and 20:1-42?

_____

_____

_____

David on the Run (1 Samuel 21–26)

7. Summarize what happens to David in Nob, as narrated in 21:1-9.

_____

_____

_____

_____

Nob (21:1). The tabernacle, the table of consecrated bread, some ninety priests, the high priest, and his ephod were all definitely at Nob at this time (see 21:1,4; 22:17-18,20; 23:6). However, the ark remained at an obscure house in Kiriath Jearim (see 1 Samuel 7:1; 2 Samuel 6:2-3).

Ahimelek (21:1). Eli's great-grandson, now high priest (see 14:3; 22:12). Compare 2:31 to 22:18.

Consecrated bread (21:4). "The bread of the Presence" (see Exodus 25:30; Leviticus 24:5-9; 1 Samuel 21:6) or "shew bread" (KJV) was twelve loaves that were placed each week in the Holy Place of the tabernacle. They were a thank offering for the provision of daily bread, consecrating the fruit of Israel's labors. "Presence" refers to God's presence as provider and Lord. When the week-old loaves were replaced with fresh ones, only the priests could eat them. Ahimelek stretched the law to let David's men have them if the men were ceremonially clean by abstaining from sex (see Exodus 19:15; Leviticus 15:18).

8. Summarize what happens to David in Gath, as narrated in 21:10-15.

_____

_____

_____

9. Summarize what happened to David in Adullam and Mizpah, as narrated in 22:1-5.

_____

_____

_____

Moab (22:3). The Moabites were descendants of Lot, Abraham's nephew (see Genesis 19:36-38), and lived east of the Dead Sea. They were usually hostile to Israel (see Numbers 22–24; Judges 3:12-30). David may have been able to find refuge for his parents there because Saul had fought the Moabites (see 1 Samuel 14:47) and the king of Moab knew of the strife between Saul and David. Also, David's great-grandmother was a Moabitess (see Ruth 4:13,22).

---

10. Which elements of Israelite society associated themselves with David at this time, according to 22:1-5 and 22:20-23? Why did these people join David?

_____

_____

_____

11. As Saul interrogated his men about David's whereabouts (see 22:6-8), to what motives did he appeal?

_____

_____

_____

For Further Study: Compare 22:1 and 24:3 with the situation described in the heading to Psalms 57 and 142. In what ways does the content of Psalms 57 and 142 appear to reflect David's circumstances and spiritual condition in 1 Samuel 22–24?

For Thought and Discussion: What significance do you see in David's concern for his parents, as indicated in 22:3-4?

Optional Application: Although under great pressure and danger, David found time to help others. Ask the Lord to help you notice others' needs and find ways to assist them.

For Further Study: What do the following passages tell us about the prophet Gad's service to David: 2 Samuel 24:11-25; 2 Chronicles 29:25,29?

For Further Study:
Compare 22:9-19
with the situation
described in the
heading to Psalm 52.
In what ways does
the content of Psalm
52 appear to reflect
David's circumstances
and spiritual con-
dition in 1 Samuel 22?

For Further Study: In
light of Deuteronomy
17:14-20 and 19:15-21,
how would you cri-
tique Saul's actions in
1 Samuel 22:13-19?

**For Thought and
Discussion:** What
factors led to the
slaughter of the
priests of Nob?

12. When summoned and accused by Saul, how did
    Ahimelek defend his actions (see 22:14-15)?

    _____

    _____

    _____

13. What is revealed about David in 22:20-22?

    _____

    _____

    _____

14. What contrasts do you see between Saul's
    treatment of Nob in chapter 22 and his actions
    toward Amalek in chapter 15? What does this
    difference reveal about Saul's priorities?

    _____

    _____

    _____

15. From 23:1-6, summarize what caused David
    and his men to go rescue the town of Keilah.
    What does the Keilah passage (see 23:1-6) tell
    us about David? What is revealed about God in
    23:1-6?

    _____

    _____

    _____

    _____

Looting the threshing floors (23:1). The Philis-
    tines apparently waited until after the Israelites
    had harvested the wheat and finished the labo-
    rious task of threshing (separating the grain
    from the stalks on which it had grown). Then
    they would come and carry off just the grain by
    force. Thus, the Israelites would have nothing
    to show for all their work.

David inquired of the Lord (23:2,4). "It is not clear how David inquired of the Lord, since Abiathar did not come until David was already in Keilah (v.6). Perhaps he inquired through the prophet Gad (see 22:5), or directly in prayer."[2] (See also 1 Samuel 30:8; 2 Samuel 2:1; 5:19,23.)

16. Summarize the major details in Saul's pursuit of David as narrated in 23:7-29. What impression do these events give of Saul? What impression do they give you of David?

_____

_____

_____

_____

_____

Six hundred (23:13). The number has increased since 22:2.

17. How is David sustained and helped in his flight from Saul, according to these passages?

23:9-13

_____

_____

23:14

_____

_____

23:15-18

_____

_____

Optional Application: In 1 and 2 Samuel, we repeatedly read that David "inquired of the Lord." "Let us learn through all of life to go to the Lord, especially when we are facing an important decision. Let us find out what is to be done, and let us not be so self-assured that we fail to pray God to show us what is useful and expedient."[3] In your life, what decisions or circumstances make it appropriate now to "inquire of the Lord"?

For Further Study: Compare 23:14-15 with the situation described in the heading to Psalm 63. In what ways does the content of Psalm 63 appear to reflect David's circumstances and spiritual condition in 1 Samuel 23?

For Further Study: Compare 23:19 with the situation described in the heading to Psalm 54. In what ways does the content of Psalm 54 appear to reflect David's circumstances and spiritual condition in 1 Samuel 23?

For Thought and Discussion: What was David risking, and what did he hope to gain, by saving Saul as he did in chapters 24 and 26?

Optional Application: Note again David's attitude of doing no violence to "the LORD's anointed" (see 24:6,10; 26:9-11). Does this serve as an example for anything in our lives today as Christians?

23:19-29

_____

_____

18. What significance do you see in David's encounter with Jonathan in 23:16-18?

_____

_____

_____

I will be second to you (23:17). "Jonathan was totally devoted to David's becoming king of Israel. . . . That statement—'I will be second'—epitomizes Jonathan's whole approach to life in the kingdom."[4]

The day the LORD spoke of when he said to you, 'I will give your enemy into your hands' (24:4). In a comparable situation in chapter 26, a similar comment is made by David's military leader Abishai (see 26:8).

"This passage raises the question . . . How is the kingdom to come into David's hands? Will he wait for it to come as Yahweh's gift or seize it by his own initiative?"[5]

19. What special significance do you see in David's words in 24:6 (repeated in verse 10) as well as in 26:9-11?

_____

_____

_____

_____

"The sanctity of Yahweh's anointed king had the status of dogma for David. This sacred respect for Saul in his official capacity was the principle that controlled David in 1 Samuel 24 and 26 (see especially 26:10-11) and kept him from regarding temptation as opportunity."[6]

For Further Study:
What do you learn by comparing David's actions toward Nabal with the following passages: Matthew 6:12-15; 18:15-35; Ephesians 4:32; Colossians 3:13?

20. What does Saul acknowledge about David's future in 24:20?

_____

_____

"Yahweh's promise of the kingdom to David . . . hangs . . . as a foregone conclusion over an almost resigned Saul (1 Samuel 24:20-21; 26:25)."[7]

21. As we see Samuel's life come to an end (in 25:1), what do you see as the most important lessons to learn from this prophet's life and ministry?

_____

_____

_____

_____

22. From 25:2-12, summarize the background and details of the encounter David's men had with Nabal. Summarize what this led to in 25:13-22.

_____

_____

_____

_____

For Further Study:
What do we learn about the right way to regard and treat our "enemies" in these passages: Exodus 23:4-5; Leviticus 19:17-18; Deuteronomy 32:35; Matthew 5:43-48; Romans 12:19; Hebrews 10:30?

Sheep-shearing time . . . a festive time (25:7-8). The counting of the sheep before shearing "would have shown how well the flocks had fared during the recent grazing," and shearing meant income soon. "David was hoping that Nabal would be in a mood to repay past favors."[8] David and his men had protected Nabal's sheep from pillage during the grazing months (see 25:7,15-16,21).

23. What are the most important details in David's encounter with Abigail in 25:23-35? What do these events lead to in 25:36-38?

24. What is significant in David's further encounter with Abigail in 25:39-42?

"Yahweh's promise of the kingdom to David . . . is assumed by both David's friends (1 Samuel 23:16-17; 25:30-31) and his opponents (2 Samuel 3:9-10,18)."[9]

25. Why do you think God twice gave David a chance to kill Saul? (Consider what David and Saul say to each other in 26:17-25, and what you observed about David in 25:1-44.)

Abishai (26:6). David's nephew (see 1 Chronicles 2:16).

Accept an offering (26:19). David suggests that if he has unknowingly wronged Saul, the matter could be settled between him and God, without Saul's taking personal revenge.

The Lord's inheritance (26:19). This is a key concept in the Old Testament. It includes both the Lord's people and His land (see Exodus 15:17; 34:9). David has been excluded from fellowship with God's people and enjoyment of His land. Even worse, the Israelites believed that to be expelled from the place of God's tabernacle and lawful sacrifices doomed a man to worship the gods of whatever land he settled in.[10]

26. How would you say the monarchy has affected Israel so far? How well is it succeeding?

_____

_____

_____

_____

Lesson Overview

27. How do you most clearly see God's sovereign control of the events in these chapters?

_____

_____

_____

28. In 1 Samuel 19–26, what confirmation do you see that David truly was a man after God's own heart (as he's described in 1 Samuel 13:14; Acts 13:22)? What evidence here helps us understand what that description means?

_____

_____

_____

_____

29. What would you select as the key verse or passage in 1 Samuel 19–26 — one that best captures or reflects the dynamics of what these chapters are all about?

_____

_____

_____

30. List any lingering questions you have about 1 Samuel 19–26.

_____

_____

_____

_____

For the Group

You may want to focus part of your discussion for lesson 4 on the following overall key themes from 1 Samuel. How do you see these themes developing in chapters 19–26? What additional recurring themes do you notice?

- Divine providence — God's sovereign oversight of human and national destiny
- The destructive effects of sin
- Obedience to God
- The kingdom of God
- Leadership
- Defining success and failure

The following numbered questions in lesson 4 may stimulate your best and most helpful discussion: 5, 6, 13, 17, 19, 21, 26, 27, 28, 29, and 30.

Remember to look also at the "For Thought and Discussion" questions in the margin.

1. *NIV Study Bible* (Grand Rapids, MI: Zondervan, 1985), on 1 Samuel 20:30.
2. *ESV Study Bible* (Wheaton, IL: Crossway, 2008), on 1 Samuel 23:2.
3. John Calvin, *Sermons on 2 Samuel*, trans. Douglas Kelly (Edinburgh, Scotland: Banner of Truth, 1992), 53, quoted in Dale Ralph Davis, *2 Samuel: Out of Every Adversity*, Focus on the Bible Commentary Series (Fearn, Scotland: Christian Focus, 1999), 31.
4. Davis, 29.
5. Davis, 14.
6. Davis, 18.
7. Davis, 60–61.
8. Robert P. Gordon, *1 and 2 Samuel* (Exeter, England: Paternoster, 1986), 182.
9. Davis, 60–61.
10. *NIV Study Bible*, on 1 Samuel 26:19.

1 SAMUEL 27–31

Further Flight and Battle

David Goes Farther Away

(1 Samuel 27)

1. What are your impressions of David's experience among the Philistines as narrated in chapter 27 and in 28:1-2? Do you think David's move into Philistine territory (see 27:1) reflects a lack of faith in the Lord? Why or why not?

   _____

   _____

   _____

2. Why do you suppose David now felt comfortable moving to Gath (see 27:2-3), although previously he had feared for his life there (see 21:10-15)? What had changed?

   _____

   _____

   _____

Geshurites ... Girzites ... Amalekites (27:8). Three pagan groups whom Israel failed to conquer under Joshua (see Joshua 13:1-3). Exterminating the pagans conformed to the instructions God gave Moses and Joshua

For Thought and Discussion: In what ways were David's words to Achish (see 28:2; 29:8) ambiguous and deceptive? Was he right to act this way?

Optional Application: God cared for David while in foreign territory and guarded him from sinning because he genuinely wanted to seek God's honor and His people's good. Can you rely on God's care and guarding in your own life? What should you do in light of this?

(see Deuteronomy 7:1-2; Joshua 6:21), although David did it for other reasons as well (see 1 Samuel 27:11).

3. How did David support himself while living in Achish's territory (see 27:8-9)?

_____

_____

_____

Negev of . . . (27:10). David told Achish that he was raiding Israelites, when he was really raiding their enemies.

4. Why did David lie to Achish about his activities (see 27:10-12)?

_____

_____

_____

You must understand (28:1). "In the ancient Near East, to accept sanctuary in a country involved obligations of military service."[1]

Saul Sinks Lower (1 Samuel 28)

5. Summarize the military situation as presented in 28:1-5.

_____

_____

_____

_____

Saul had expelled the mediums and spiritists from the land (28:3). This may mean he'd had them executed unless they managed to flee the country (see 28:9,21). The Law commanded that occult practitioners be executed (see Leviticus 19:31; 20:6,27; Deuteronomy 18:11). This statement illustrates that much more happened during Saul's reign than is included in the books of Samuel (compare 2 Samuel 21:1-2). The author selected only those details that were essential to the themes God wanted to convey.

For Thought and Discussion: How does a Christian inquire of the Lord? What are the right methods?

For Thought and Discussion: Why does the Lord detest mediums and spiritists?

6. What problems did Saul face at this time, as indicated in 28:3-6?

_____

_____

_____

_____

Dreams or Urim or prophets (28:6). Saul normally sought guidance from the Lord both by personal revelation and by the agency of priests and prophets. David had a prophet, but no prophet served Saul. Likewise, David's priest Abiathar had the ephod with the Urim and Thummin. Saul may have had copies of the lots made, or the author of 1 Samuel may be speaking idiomatically of the three usual ways of inquiring of the Lord.

7. In 28:6-11, how did Saul respond to the military situation?

_____

_____

_____

8. Why do you think Saul sought to contact Samuel?

_____

_____

_____

The woman saw Samuel (28:12). "Probably this
was Samuel, and not merely an apparition. The
consternation of the medium shows that the
figure was something outside her usual experience of magic arts. The narrator calls it simply
'Samuel,' and what the figure says is consistent
with Samuel's pronouncements when alive
(especially chapter 15). For some reason the
Lord allowed Samuel to visit Saul. It is clear
from the medium's reaction that she could not
compel him to appear."[2] "Whatever the explanation of this mysterious affair, the medium
was used in some way to convey to Saul that
the impending battle would bring death, would
dash his hopes for a dynasty, and would conclude his reign with a devastating defeat of
Israel that would leave the nation at the mercy
of the Philistines, the very people against whom
he had struggled all his years as king."[3]

---

9. a. In 28:12-19, what does Saul learn? How does
this information conform to what Samuel
told Saul earlier in 15:26-28?

_____

_____

_____

b. In 28:20-25, how does Saul respond to this
information?

_____

_____

_____

10. How does what Samuel says to Saul in chapter
28 compare to what the Lord revealed to Eli
through Samuel in chapter 3?

_____

_____

_____

11. What does this whole episode, including Saul's final reaction, reveal about his psychological and spiritual state?

_____

_____

_____

Saul's End (1 Samuel 29–31)

12. Summarize the events and military develop-ments occurring in chapter 29. What are your impressions of David in this chapter?

_____

_____

_____

13. a. What is the situation confronting David in 30:1-6? Why was his situation especially des-perate, as evidenced in 30:5-6?

_____

_____

_____

b. What is the significance of David's response to this crisis in 30:6? How does David further respond in 30:7-8?

_____

_____

_____

14. While pursuing the enemy, what act of mercy did David and his men perform (see 30:11-15)? How was their kindness rewarded?

For Further Study:
How would you com-pare David's trial in 1 Samuel 30:6 with the ordeal of Moses in Numbers 14:1-10?

Optional Application: Exiled, bereft of his family and his goods, threat-ened with the mutiny of his troops, and without the comfort and counsel of his friend Jonathan and mentor Samuel, David in 30:6 had only the Lord between him and despair. Are you able to depend only on the Lord in times of trial? How can you do this in your current situation?

Optional Application: For believers today, what possible application might 1 Samuel 30 have to our daily spiritual warfare?

15. a. Summarize the events and military developments unfolding in 30:9-20.

    b. What further tension does this lead to in 30:21-25, and how does David resolve the tension?

16. What is the significance of David's actions in 30:26-31?

For 1 Samuel 31, see the parallel account in 1 Chronicles 10:1-12.

17. In his last battle with the Philistines, what tragedies did Saul witness before his death, according to 31:1-2?

18. How did Saul die, according to 31:3-6? What do you think the author of 1 Samuel (and the Holy Spirit) wanted to emphasize about Saul in the account of how he died?

_____

_____

_____

_____

19. In 31:11-13, why did the citizens of Jabesh Gilead risk their lives to recover Saul's body and bury his bones? (Recall 11:1-11.) What does this act say about them?

_____

_____

_____

_____

20. How does Israel's situation at the end of chapter 31 compare with its situation at the end of chapter 4?

_____

_____

_____

_____

21. As we see Saul's life come to an end, what do you see as the most important lessons to learn from his life? What were the ultimate consequences of Saul's reign for Israel?

_____

_____

_____

_____

_____

For Thought and Discussion: What does chapter 31 reveal about Israel's request for a king in chapter 8?

For Thought and Discussion: How did Saul's disobedience affect him and others? How is this relevant to you?

For Thought and Discussion: Which aspects of God's character challenged you the most as you studied 1 Samuel?

For Thought and Discussion: What is the relationship between obedience and victory in 1 Samuel? Does this principle operate in the lives of Christians today? If so, how and to what extent? If not, why not?

85

For Further Study:
From what you see
in the Gospels, how
does Jesus, in His life
and ministry, show
us more clearly the
qualities of "a man
after God's own
heart"?

**Optional
Application:** Which
verses in 1 Samuel
would be most
helpful for you to
memorize, so you
have them always
available in your mind
and heart for the Holy
Spirit to use?

Lesson Overview

22. In 1 Samuel 27–31, what confirmation do you
    see that David was truly a man after God's own
    heart (see 1 Samuel 13:14; Acts 13:22)? And
    what evidence here helps us understand what
    that description means?

    _____

    _____

    _____

    _____

23. What would you select as the key verse or
    passage in 1 Samuel 27–31 — one that best
    captures or reflects the dynamics of what these
    chapters are all about?

    _____

    _____

    _____

    _____

24. List any lingering questions you have about
    1 Samuel 27–31.

    _____

    _____

    _____

Reviewing 1 Samuel

25. How do you most clearly see God's sovereign
    control of the events in 1 Samuel?

    _____

    _____

    _____

    _____

26. From all that you've seen in 1 Samuel, how would you summarize the most important developments in David's preparation for serving as Israel's king? What do these chapters reveal about David's gifts and abilities as a future leader of all God's people?

_____

_____

_____

_____

27. What do you see as the most important themes that have emerged in 1 Samuel?

_____

_____

_____

_____

For the Group

You may want to focus part of your discussion for lesson 5 on the following overall key themes from 1 Samuel. How do you see these themes developing in chapters 27–31? What other recurring themes have you detected?

- Divine providence — God's sovereign oversight of human and national destiny
- The destructive effects of sin
- Obedience to God
- The kingdom of God
- Leadership
- Defining success and failure

The following numbered questions in lesson 5 may stimulate your best and most helpful discussion: 13, 15, 18, 20, 21, 22, 23, and 24.

Allow enough discussion time to look back together and review all of 1 Samuel as a whole. You can use questions 25, 26, and 27 in this lesson to help you do that.

Look also at the questions in the margin under the heading "For Thought and Discussion."

1. *NIV Study Bible* (Grand Rapids, MI: Zondervan, 1985), on 1 Samuel 28:1.
2. *New Geneva Study Bible* (Nashville: Thomas Nelson, 1995), on 1 Samuel 28:12.
3. *NIV Study Bible*, on 1 Samuel 28:12.

2 SAMUEL

A Kingdom in Crisis

"Like 1 Samuel, this book is a historical chronicle that uses literary resources for telling a nation's history. Considered in the ancient context that produced the book, it can be called court history, meaning that its chief subject matter is the history of what happened at court (where the king was the dominant figure), recorded by official court historians."[1]

Although the books of 1 and 2 Samuel form a unified account, in 2 Samuel we see a definite narrowing of focus: "Whereas 1 Samuel focused on several major characteristics, from start to finish 2 Samuel belongs to the central heroic figure of David. The author was obviously privy to personal information about David in addition to his actions in the public and political spheres. Throughout, we need to pay attention to the ways in which God is a leading actor in the story."[2]

By centering on David and his extraordinary life, the book makes for a compelling read. "David is one of the most colorful characters in the Bible — a bigger-than-life figure of heroic accomplishments and passions. The strategy of the author of 2 Samuel is to build virtually everything around this heroic figure."[3]

"The presence of David as the engaging central character is the primary unifying focus of this collection of stories. The world of the story also unifies the book: it is a political and courtly world, a military world, a religious world, and a domestic world. Two threads of action make up the story of David's heroic life — the public life of a king and the personal life of a family man."[4]

What those story threads reveal is remarkably realistic. David's life is marked by profound tragedy, but the tragedy does not finally overcome. "Second Samuel is the prose epic of David, telling the story of a nation led by a heroic leader. It is at the same time a hero story in which the protagonist, while not wholly idealized, is nonetheless a largely exemplary and representative character who embodies the struggles and ideals of his society."[5]

The narrative's realism ultimately compels us to see the higher hand that is obviously at work in directing a story filled with such incredible happenings. "Again and again as we read 2 Samuel we have to shake ourselves and say, 'This is not about David; it is not even about covenant kings; it is about a covenant God who makes covenant promises to a covenant king through whom he will preserve his covenant people.' That must be our perspective."[6]

That perspective inevitably turns our attention to the future. The true triumph of David comes only in the story of the Son of David, Jesus Christ—who would come to earth to gain David's throne forever (see Luke 1:32).

1. Leland Ryken and Philip Graham Ryken, eds., *The Literary Study Bible* (Wheaton, IL: Crossway, 2007), introduction to 2 Samuel, "The Book at a Glance."
2. Ryken and Ryken, "The Book at a Glance."
3. Ryken and Ryken, "Storytelling Technique."
4. Ryken and Ryken, "Unifying Elements."
5. *ESV Study Bible* (Wheaton, IL: Crossway, 2008), introduction to 1–2 Samuel: "Literary Features."
6. Dale Ralph Davis, *2 Samuel: Out of Every Adversity*, Focus on the Bible Commentary Series (Fearn, Scotland: Christian Focus, 1999), 9.

2 SAMUEL 1–5

The Chosen King Enthroned

1. God says that His Word is like fire and like a hammer (see Jeremiah 23:29). He can use His Word to burn away unclean thoughts and desires in our hearts. He can use it with hammer-like hardness to crush and crumble our spiritual hardness. As you continue your study in the books of 1 and 2 Samuel, how do you most want to see the "fire-and-hammer" power of God's Word at work in your own life? Again, express this longing in a written prayer to God.

_____

_____

_____

_____

_____

2. Think about these words of Paul to his younger helper Timothy: "Do your best to present yourself to God as one approved, a worker who does not need to be ashamed and who correctly handles the word of truth" (2 Timothy 2:15). Remember once more that getting the most from your study will take concentration and perseverance. Express here your commitment before God to work diligently as you go on to complete your study of 1 and 2 Samuel, that you may "present yourself to God as one approved."

Optional Application: Recall again how Jesus explained Old Testament passages to His disciples, as He "opened their minds so they could understand the Scriptures" (Luke 24:45). Ask God to do that kind of work in *your* mind as you study 2 Samuel, so you're released and free to learn everything here He wants you to learn — and so you can become as bold and worshipful and faithful as those early disciples of Jesus were. Express this desire to Him in prayer.

_____

_____

_____

_____

3. In one sitting if possible, read over the first five chapters of 2 Samuel. What two or three things stand out most to you from your reading?

_____

_____

_____

_____

4. From chapters 1–5 in 2 Samuel, summarize the most important factors and developments allowing David to be firmly established as king over all Israel.

_____

_____

_____

_____

David Mourns (2 Samuel 1)

5. a. From 2 Samuel 1:1-10, summarize the circumstances in which David learns of the deaths of Saul and Jonathan.

_____

_____

_____

b. How would you describe David's reaction to this news as seen in 1:11-27?

_____

_____

_____

The LORD's anointed (1:14). See also 1 Samuel
24:6,10 and 26:9-11.

Why weren't you afraid (1:14). "David's question
expresses a principle that should direct all kingdom ethics and behavior. There is in kingdom
living such a thing as healthy, saving fear; a
fear that preserves, a godly fear that should
control us."[1]

6. Summarize the differences you see between the
Amalekite's version of how Saul died (see 1:6-10)
and the narrative given earlier in 1 Samuel 31?

_____

_____

_____

_____

In the Amalekite's account of Saul's death (see
1:6-10), we're immediately confronted with
a description that differs from what we read
at the end of 1 Samuel 31. "The solution is
simple: the Amalekite lied. If you ever have a
choice between the narrator and an Amalekite,
always believe the narrator. Have you ever met
an Amalekite you could trust?"[2]

Strike him down! (1:15). "The Amalekite received
justice (verses 15-16), but it is justice mixed
with irony. He is punished for what he said he
did even though (in our view) he didn't do it!
He received what he should have received even
though it was not based on fact. The judgment
of God . . . found him in his lie and repaid him
in line with his intent if not his deed. . . . In
Yahweh's kingdom we have to do with a God
who sees, exposes, and judges. . . . What you
see in 2 Samuel 1 in the Amalekite's case is a
preview of what will be true for all at the last
day. 'There is _nothing_ concealed that will not
be disclosed.'"[3]

Notice in chapter 1 that verses 11 and 12, which record the lasting grief of David and his men, are inserted *before* the continuation of David's conversation with the Amalekite messenger (in verses 13-14) and the account of David's immediate dealings with the messenger. "For our writer . . . the most important item in his story is the grief and wailing of David and his men over Israel — her fallen leaders and troops. The 'people of Yahweh' have been crushed. Grief cannot wait. . . . Nothing else matters, except giving vent to this anguish."[4]

7. What does 2 Samuel 1:19-27 reveal about David's deepest attitudes and feelings toward Saul and Jonathan?

_____

_____

_____

"Grief . . . abides. And because it abides there must be some mechanism, some procedures, by which God's people can express that grief. That is what David does in this passage; in his lament over Israel, Saul, and Jonathan, he provides a vehicle by which Israel can continue her mourning."[5]

This lament (1:17). "David . . . produced a self-conscious, reflective expression of grief that could be reduced to written form. . . . A lament . . . is a vehicle for the mind as well as for the emotions. A lament is an expression of *thoughtful* grief. . . . The intensity of one's emotions unite with the discipline of one's mind to produce structured sorrow, a sort of authorized version of distress, a kind of coherent agony. In a lament, therefore, words are carefully

94

selected, crafted, honed to express loss as closely yet fully as possible."

Ordered that the people of Judah be taught this lament (1:18). "David wanted the fighting men of his own tribe to know this sad song, to know it by heart, to have it crammed into their pores. But why? Why should troops learn poetry? Why should the army of Judah always have the lyrics of defeat ringing in their ears? Because David intends it as part of their motivational military training. Gilboa was not the last time Israel would fight Philistines — and David wanted his men to remember Gilboa, to remember the tragedy, remember the pagan arrogance. He wanted them deeply stirred and moved — for the next time."[6]

Lament of the bow (1:18). "The Bow" may be David's title for this lament, in reference to the mention of Jonathan's bow in verse 22. (See Jonathan's gift to David of a bow in 1 Samuel 18:4).

A gazelle lies slain (1:19). Referring likely to Jonathan and Saul, and perhaps chiefly to Jonathan (see the parallel construction in verse 25).

8. In his lament, what specific qualities of Jonathan and Saul does David praise, and why do you think these are uppermost in David's mind?

_____

_____

_____

_____

"In no uncertain terms verses 22-23 summarize the bravery, the determination, the comradeship, and the ability of King Saul and his son Jonathan."[7]

Saul and Jonathan . . . in death they were not parted (1:23). The friendship between Jonathan and David "never swayed Jonathan from loyalty to his father or from standing beside him at the last."[8]

Swifter than eagles . . . stronger than lions (1:23). "Ironically, the other two places in the Old Testament where 'swift' and 'strong' are parallel . . . may be applied to the tragic end of Saul and Jonathan: 'The race is not to the swift/or the battle to the strong' (Ecclesiastes 9:11); 'The swift cannot flee/nor the strong escape' (Jeremiah 46:6)."[9]

I grieve for you, Jonathan my brother. . . . Your love for me was wonderful (1:26). "David knows he has lost the friend *par excellence.* . . . 'The more we love the more we grieve' (Matthew Henry). Sorrow will be hardest where love is deepest."[10]

Rival Kings (2 Samuel 2–3)

David inquired of the Lᴏʀᴅ (2:1). See also 1 Samuel 23:2,4; 30:8; 2 Samuel 5:19,23. "Even though David clearly knew that God had constituted him as king and that Saul had trespassed, even though the time was ripe for him to enjoy the crown, nevertheless he asked God to tell him what he should do? Why? Because although he was on the way, he still knew that he could err seriously if God did not guide him."[11]

To Hebron (2:1). "David has broken completely with Philistia and has made a new beginning in Judah. . . . Yahweh authorizes David to leave Ziklag for Judah and for Hebron in particular"; Hebron was "the most important town in Judah. Here the men of Judah 'anointed David king over the tribe of Judah' (verse 4). Here the kingdom of God becomes visible in the world—for those who have eyes to see. . . . Here, for the first time, Yahweh's chosen king

visibly rules on earth. . . . It is a small beginning, but it is the kingdom of God —
concrete, visible, earthy."[12]

For Further Study:
In the following
passages, notice
the rich history that
Hebron would hold
for David and for all
Israel: Genesis 13:18;
23:2,17-19; 25:9-10;
49:29-32; 50:13;
Joshua 15:13-14.

9. What contrasts do you see in chapter 2 between
how David was made king and how Ish-Bosheth
was?

_____

_____

_____

10. What significance do you see in how David
reached out (in 2:4-7) to the people of Jabesh
Gilead? (Refer to 1 Samuel 11 to review how
Saul had earlier rescued that city from the
Ammonites; see also 1 Samuel 31:11-13.)

_____

_____

_____

"The promotion of Ishbosheth as king
was not only a continuation of the
hostility of Saul towards David, but also
an open act of rebellion against Jehovah,
who had rejected Saul and chosen David
prince over Israel."[13]

11. What special significance do you see in the
action reported in 2 Samuel 2:8-9?

_____

_____

_____

"Abner was opposing Yahweh's kingship
and will."[14]

97

12. How would you summarize the background, confrontation, and results in the conflict described in 2:12-32?

_____

_____

_____

_____

Asahel had fallen (2:23). "Asahel, though dead because of his headlong pursuit of Abner, would be long remembered in Israel. He is listed first among the 'Thirty,' David's military elite (23:24). . . . Asahel's untimely death early in David's reign made it necessary for his son to succeed him in that post (1 Chronicles 27:7). It would only be a matter of time, however, before Asahel's brother Joab would avenge his great loss (3:30)."[15]

The war . . . lasted a long time (3:1). "War—almost inevitable when rivals aspire to the same throne—continues between them. . . . But Ish-Bosheth's weakness is no match for David's strength, and the outcome is a foregone conclusion. Indeed, as if to emphasize David's invincible, divinely given power (see 5:10), the narrator pits David alone, who 'grew stronger and stronger,' against the entire 'house of Saul,' who 'grew weaker and weaker.'"[16]

Sons were born to David in Hebron (3:2). "His firstborn son Amnon, the son of Ahinoam, would ultimately be killed by the men of Absalom (13:28-29), David's third son (verse 3). His second son, Kileab, whose mother was Abigail (verse 3), is mentioned only here and apparently died before he was able to enter the fray to determine who would be David's successor as king of Israel. . . . Adonijah (verse 4) would figure prominently in the struggle for David's throne (see 1 Kings 1–2), eventually to be assassinated in favor of Solomon. Of Shephatiah . . . and of Ithream . . . nothing further is known."[17]

For 2 Samuel 3:2-5, see the parallel account in 1 Chronicles 3:1-4.

"The story of how David became king of all Israel follows, in most essentials, the same outline already established in the account of his accession to kingship over Judah (1:1–3:5). . . . The similarities between the two sections point to the careful craftsmanship of a single author, who now sets about to tell his readers that just as the house of David has replaced Saul and his house in southern Canaan (1:1–3:5), so also David's house is about to replace that of Saul in the rest of the land as well (3:6–5:16)."[18]

Note the similar structure and order of these two accounts in the chart below.[19]

	David's reign established over Judah	David's reign established over all Israel
"a warrior trying to curry David's favor"	1:1-13	3:6-21
"the execution or murder of the warrior"	1:14-16	3:22-32
"a lament uttered by David"	1:17-27	3:33-34
"a brief report of the anointing of David as king"	2:1-7	5:1-5
"David and his men are then successful in defeating their enemies"	2:8–3:1	5:6-12
"a list of sons/ children born to David"	3:2-5	5:13-16

13. a. Summarize the events in chapter 3 involving Abner. What is the significance of these events, both for David and for Israel?

_____

_____

_____

    b. What do these events demonstrate about
       Abner's character and personality?

_____

_____

_____

14. What does Abner understand about God's plan
    for David, according to 2 Samuel 3:9-10 and
    3:18?

_____

_____

_____

David's throne (3:10). This throne, "already
    established over Judah (2:4) and soon to be
    established over Israel, would some day soon
    be occupied by David's son Solomon (1 Kings
    2:12,24,45), later be discredited by Solomon's
    reprobate descendants who would be destroyed
    by the Lord himself (Jeremiah 13:13-14; 29:16-
    17), and eventually be inherited by the Lord's
    Messiah, who will reign forever in peace and
    with justice and righteousness (Isaiah 9:6-7)."[20]

"Since Abner clearly knew that Yahweh
had promised David the kingship (3:9-10,
17-18), his armed resistance seems baffling. But for anyone who looks at
humanity and history through the doctrine of original sin, it is not baffling at all.
Only perverse. . . . Abner is not far from
any of us. We share an Abner-nature
that harbors sin's stupidity, perversity,

and twistedness. Let Abner preach to you. Let him tell you that it is possible to know the truth but not embrace the truth, to quote the truth but not submit to the truth, to hold the truth and yet assault the truth."[21]

My servant David (3:18). More than thirty times in the Old Testament, David is called the Lord's "servant."

All Israel . . . all that your heart desires (3:21). The northern tribes of Israel will be added to Judah under David's kingship. Two generations later, Israel and Judah will be divided again (this time permanently), and the authority of David's dynasty will again be limited to Judah. Ironically, at that time, the phrase "all that your heart desires" will be spoken by God's prophet Ahijah to the rebel leader Jeroboam in reference to the northern tribes' rising up against David's grandson, Rehoboam.

---

15. What does chapter 3 reveal about the personality and character of Joab?

_____

_____

_____

_____

"It is likely . . . that Joab smelled a rival in Abner and that he feared Abner might replace him as commander of the army. That could well have been in the works as part of David's deal with Abner (3:12-13)."[22]

He went in peace (3:21). "We are told three times
that David dismissed Abner and that Abner
'went in peace' (verses 21,22,23). This likely
means that he had been granted safe conduct;
'in peace' means 'in security.' All of which
explains why Abner returned so unsuspectingly
to Hebron. . . . Why should he be suspicious?
He never saw Joab's dagger until it was too
late—it had been concealed behind David's
promise. Hence Joab committed the most
sinister form of treachery."[23]

16. What explanation would you give to David's
words and actions in 3:31-38?

_____

_____

_____

Everything the king did pleased them (3:36).
"The remarkable result of God's blessing on
these initial days of David's reign."[24]

David's Kingdom United (2 Samuel 4–5)

17. Summarize the events in 4:1-8 resulting in Ish-
Bosheth's death and the report of it to David.

_____

_____

_____

Mephibosheth (4:4). His story will be continued in
9:1-13, 16:1-4, and 19:24-30. "Mephibosheth is
introduced parenthetically to demonstrate that
his youth and physical handicap disqualify him
for rule in the north. . . . Five years old when
his father died, Mephibosheth would still have
been only twelve (see 2:11) at the time of the
assassination of his uncle Ish-Bosheth."[25]

"Rechab and Baanah . . . are only saying that by their deed they have decisively eliminated the whole threat against David from Saul's house. . . . They want to put a certain spin on their treachery to suggest that David is indebted to them for this finishing touch that makes his person and kingdom secure. And therein lurks the temptation. Are they not, however subtly, pretending to be David's redeemers to whom he owes something for coming to the kingdom? But . . . David is able to recognize them for what they are and to repudiate their claim because he remembers his true and only Redeemer."[26]

18. How does David respond in 4:9-12 to the report of Ish-Bosheth's death at the hands of Rechab and Baanah? What does this response reveal about David?

_____

_____

_____

_____

"With the death of Ish-Bosheth, no other viable candidate for king remains for the elders of the northern tribes. Meanwhile David sits in regal isolation, above the fray as always, innocent of the deaths of Saul, Jonathan, Abner, and now Ish-Bosheth. The way is open for his march to the throne of Israel."[27]

The LORD . . . has delivered me out of every trouble (4:9). "This was no flippant remark. . . . This formula . . . does not describe a mere stage or segment of David's life but his whole life. . . . He uses the *very same words* at the end of his reign (1 Kings 1:29). David and distress walked together his whole life."[28]

For the following passages in 2 Samuel 5, see parallel accounts in 1 Chronicles as listed below:

- For verses 1-3, see 1 Chronicles 11:1-3.
- For verses 4-5, see 1 Chronicles 3:4; 29:26-27 (see also 1 Kings 2:11).
- For verses 6-10, see 1 Chronicles 11:4-9.
- For verses 11-12, see 1 Chronicles 14:1-2.
- For verses 13-16, see 1 Chronicles 3:5-8; 14:3-7.
- For verses 17-25, see 1 Chronicles 14:8-16.

In 2 Samuel 5, "the various sections (verses 1-5, 6-10, 11-12, 13-16, 17-25) do not follow a strict chronological order. . . . Biblical writers are not chained to chronological order — and in 2 Samuel 5 the chains have certainly fallen off. The chapter is orderly but not sequential. It is a collage; it is a collection of fragments intending to give us a proper view of the kingdom."[29]

---

19. According to 5:2, what do the people of Israel understand about God's plan for David?

_____

_____

The LORD said to you, "You will shepherd my people Israel, and you will become their ruler" (5:2). "When the northern tribes cite Yahweh's promise at the Hebron negotiations, the writer wants us to highlight it in our text, as if to say, 'See there? See how Yahweh's promise to David has come to pass? See how it has weathered the venom of Saul (1 Samuel 18-26), the follies of

David (1 Samuel 25,27,29), the rebellion of the north (2 Samuel 2:8-32), and the self-seeking of "friends" (2 Samuel 1:1-16; 3:22-30; 4:1-12)? See how Yahweh's promise has proved firm in the face of *intense opposition,* chapters and chapters of it since 1 Samuel 18?' He implies that all Yahweh's promises are certain no matter how much resistance they may meet."[30]

20. What emphasis do you see in the account of David's campaign to conquer Jerusalem in 5:6-9?

_____

_____

_____

For Further Study: What further uses of the "shepherd" imagery for Israel's leadership do you see in these passages: Psalm 78:70-72; Jeremiah 3:15; 23:4; Ezekiel 34:23; 37:24? See also the use of this imagery for Jesus in John 10:11-14, Hebrews 13:20, and 1 Peter 5:4.

Jerusalem

"The account of David's kingship over Israel starts with the capture of Jerusalem, on the boundary between Judah and Benjamin. It had not been controlled by any tribe, and thus it was both symbolically and geographically better suited to be the capital of all Israel than Hebron (in central Judah). Jerusalem was the 'Salem' of Melchizedek (Genesis 14:18). It has been fortified since the Middle Bronze Age, i.e., the first half of the second millennium b.c. In the second half of the millennium it was one of the city-states of Canaan that was under the influence of Egypt. . . . The city was too strong to be conquered at the time of Joshua (Joshua 15:63; Judges 1:21)."[31]

"The city had earlier been conquered by Judah (Judges 1:8) but neither Judah nor Benjamin had been successful in permanently dislodging its Jebusite inhabitants."[32]

"One of the most significant accomplishments of David's reign was the establishment of Jerusalem as his royal city and the nation's capital. . . . By locating his royal city in a newly conquered town on the border between the two segments of his realm, David united the kingdom under his rule without seeming to subordinate one part to the other."[33]

105

Jebusites (5:6). See Genesis 10:16 for their origin, and 15:21 for their mention in God's promise to Abraham of a homeland for his descendants. In later reiterating that promise, God repeatedly mentioned the Jebusites to Moses at the burning bush (see Exodus 3:8,17), and to all Israel when He gave His laws to them at Mount Sinai (see Exodus 23:23; 33:2; 34:11). In Deuteronomy, Moses reminds the people that the Jebusites were among the peoples who were to be completely destroyed once Israel entered the Promised Land (see 7:1-2; 20:17). Although some Jebusites were defeated by Joshua and the army of Israel, they were not entirely wiped out (see Joshua 15:63; Judges 1:21; 3:5).

Fortress of Zion (5:7). "This marks the first occurrence of 'Zion' in the Bible and the only one in Samuel. The name originally designated a fortified mound located at the southern end of the Ophel ridge. Eventually the name came to be used in an extended sense for all of Jerusalem (2 Kings 19:21; Isaiah 2:3) and even for the entire nation of Israel (Psalm 149:2; Isaiah 46:13). The name occurs frequently in Israel's poetic and prophetic literature, where it is often presented as the place of God's mighty acts of salvation and judgment (e.g., Psalm 14:7; Isaiah 4:4; Lamentations 4:11)."[34]

The blind and the lame (5:6). "The interchange about the 'blind' and the 'lame' in verses 6 and 8, although interpreted in numerous ways . . . is best understood as an example of pre-battle verbal taunting."[35]

Those "lame and blind" who are David's enemies (5:8). "David would eventually welcome the lame Mephibosheth (9:13) into the royal palace, and in the messianic age the blind and the lame would be special recipients of divine favor (see Isaiah 35:5-6; Jeremiah 31:8; Matthew 12:22; 21:14; Acts 3:7-8)."[36]

21. What do you see as the full significance of the statement made about David in 2 Samuel 5:10?

_____

_____

_____

_____

The LORD God Almighty was with him (5:10). Look ahead also to Nathan's words to David in 7:3 and God's words to David in 7:9.

22. According to 5:12, what truth did David recognize, and what is the importance of that truth?

_____

_____

_____

_____

David knew that the LORD . . . had exalted his kingdom for the sake of his people Israel (5:12). "Yahweh did not anchor David's throne so he could act like a king but so that he could function as a servant toward his people."[37]

More sons . . . were born to him (5:13). "The first four names in the list (verse 14) are of sons born to David by Bathsheba (1 Chronicles 3:5), two of whom appear elsewhere in the biblical narratives. . . . Nathan . . . is mentioned in Luke 3:31 in the genealogy of Jesus. Solomon . . . appearing here for the first time in the Bible, and David's tenth son overall (David himself was an eighth son), would eventually outlast his rivals for the throne and rule over the united kingdom."[38]

We get a mixed picture of David in 2 Samuel 5:13-16. "On the one hand the number of David's sons indicates his strength; on the other hand, the number of his concubines and wives reveals his folly, for this practice was in direct violation of Yahweh's prescriptions for the covenant king (Deuteronomy 17:17). . . . Here is both David's strength and his stupidity. . . . Even David compromises and mars the kingdom over which he rules; ultimately, the kingdom is safe only in the hands of David's Descendant who always does what pleases the Father (John 8:29)."[39]

Concubines and wives (5:13). This is "the only time that the phrase 'concubines and wives' occurs in the Bible (the usual order is 'wives and concubines'). . . . By placing the word 'concubines' in emphatic position, the narrator is perhaps deploring David's proclivity for the trappings of a typical Oriental monarch, including a harem."[40]

23. What characteristics of how David lived his life are especially revealed in 5:17-25?

_____

_____

_____

"Although by no means the only battles King David fought against the Philistines (see 8:1), these [in 5:17-25] serve as a paradigm to summarize the continuing conflict."[41]

24. Observe how God dealt with and guided David and Israel in 5:17-25. Notice especially the demonstration here of God's *guidance* and His

108

power. What might this passage reveal about God's ways of relating with His people in all ages, including today?

_____

_____

_____

_____

As waters break out, the Lord has broken out against my enemies (5:20). "David compared Yahweh's activity to the way a massive torrent of water breaks down everything in its path. Just so Yahweh levels the opposition."[42]

The Lord has gone out in front of you to strike the Philistine army (5:24). "Yahweh styles himself as the Warrior who plunges into battle and knocks off the Philistines."[43]

"Note what vigorous images the text gives us of Yahweh's power: the Leveler and the Warrior. Contemporary Christians must not tone these down. . . . Yahweh's people have a God who is a smasher and a fighter, a God 'mighty in battle' (Psalm 24:8), who can *therefore* defend his sheep and restrain and conquer all his and our enemies."[44]

Lesson Overview

25. Remember again Scripture's emphasis that David was a man after God's own heart (see 1 Samuel 13:14; Acts 13:22). What confirmation of this do you see in 2 Samuel 1–5? What evidence here helps us understand what that description means?

Optional Application: For believers today, what application does 2 Samuel 5:17-25 have to our daily spiritual warfare?

Optional Application: Notice in 5:20 how David gave glory to God. What pattern might this show for how we can give glory to God today?

26. What would you select as the key verse or passage in 2 Samuel 1–5 — one that best captures or reflects the dynamics of what these chapters are all about?

27. List any lingering questions you have about 2 Samuel 1–5.

For the Group

You may want to focus part of your discussion for lesson 6 on the following overall key themes from 2 Samuel. How do you see these themes developing in chapters 1–5? And what other recurring themes have you noticed?

- God's covenant with His people
- Godly leadership
- Sin, repentance, and forgiveness
- Community and family

The following numbered questions in lesson 6 may stimulate your best and most helpful discussion: 3, 4, 7, 22, 23, 24, 25, 26, and 27.

Look also at the questions in the margin under the heading "For Thought and Discussion."

1. Dale Ralph Davis, *2 Samuel: Out of Every Adversity*, Focus on the Bible Commentary Series (Fearn, Scotland: Christian Focus, 1999), 18.
2. Davis, 14.
3. Davis, 15–16.
4. Davis, 17.
5. Davis, 21.
6. Davis, 26.
7. Ronald F. Youngblood, *Expositor's Bible Commentary*, ed. Frank E. Gaebelein, vol. 3, *1–2 Samuel* (Grand Rapids, MI: Zondervan, 1992), 814.
8. Davis, 28.
9. Youngblood, 814.
10. Davis, 29.
11. John Calvin, *Sermons on 2 Samuel*, trans. Douglas Kelly (Edinburgh, Scotland: Banner of Truth, 1992), 53, quoted in Davis, 31.
12. Davis, 32–33.
13. C. F. Keil, *Biblical Commentary on the Books of Samuel* (1875; repr., Grand Rapids, MI: Eerdmans 1950), 292, quoted in Davis, 36–37).
14. Davis, 37.
15. Youngblood, 827.
16. Youngblood, 828.
17. Youngblood, 830.
18. Youngblood, 831–832.
19. Adapted from Youngblood, 831.
20. Youngblood, 834.
21. Davis, 41–42.
22. Davis, 46.
23. Davis, 45.
24. *ESV Study Bible* (Wheaton, IL: Crossway, 2008), on 2 Samuel 3:36.
25. Youngblood, 844.
26. Davis, 54.
27. Youngblood, 847.
28. Davis, 9.
29. Davis, 59–60.
30. Davis, 61.
31. *ESV Study Bible*, on 2 Samuel 5:6-13.
32. *New Geneva Study Bible* (Nashville: Thomas Nelson, 1995), on 2 Samuel 5:6.
33. *NIV Study Bible* (Grand Rapids, MI: Zondervan, 1985), on 2 Samuel 5:6.
34. *New Geneva Study Bible*, on 2 Samuel 5:7.
35. Youngblood, 854–855.
36. Youngblood, 856.
37. Davis, 65.

38. Youngblood, 860.
39. Davis, 66.
40. Youngblood, 859.
41. Youngblood, 862.
42. Davis, 68.
43. Davis, 68.
44. Davis, 68–69.

2 SAMUEL 6–9

A Covenant Forever

The Ark Restored (2 Samuel 6)

For the following passages in 2 Samuel 6, see parallel accounts in 1 Chronicles as listed below:

- For verses 1-11, see 1 Chronicles 13:5-14.
- For verses 12-19, see 1 Chronicles 15:25–16:3.
- For verses 19-20, see 1 Chronicles 16:43.

For Further Study:
What do you learn about the ark and its significance in these passages: Exodus 25:10-22; Leviticus 16:14-15; Numbers 10:35-36; Deuteronomy 10:1-5; 1 Chronicles 28:2?

1. How does the description of the ark in 6:2 highlight its importance?

_____

_____

_____

_____

2. Summarize all that was done in chapter 6 in regard to the ark of God.

_____

_____

_____

_____

_____

"By bringing the ark to Zion, David is saying that Yahweh's presence can no longer remain, so to speak, on a side rail (see 1 Chronicles 13:3) but must be the central focus and reality of the Davidic kingdom. The worship of Yahweh, this ruling, reconciling, revealing God, must be at the heart of Israel's life. The ark in Jerusalem proclaims that the majestic, pardoning, speaking God is in the midst of his people."[1]

3. In 6:3-4, notice the manner in which the ark was carried. Compare with the regulations given for this in Exodus 25:14-15; Numbers 4:4-6,15,17-20; 7:9; Deuteronomy 10:8; 31:9,25. What differences do you see?

_____

_____

_____

_____

"The rules were: no touch, no look, no cart. The priests were to cover the sacred furniture after which they would assign Levites of the Kohathite clan to carry such items (hence, implicitly, no carts). The Kohathites were not to touch or look upon the sacred items 'lest they die' (Numbers 4:15,20). Clearly, Yahweh did not want them to die; his _kindness_ was written all over that warning. So it was not as though David and Uzzah and company had had no warning. Yahweh's blow was scarcely arbitrary."[2]

4. a. How would you explain what happens to Uzzah in 6:6-7, and why? (See also 1 Chronicles 15:13.)

_____

_____

b. What is significant about David's reaction to this in 6:8-10?

_____

_____

_____

For Further Study:
How is the God we meet in 2 Samuel 6:5-10 shown to be the same God we meet in the New Testament? See Acts 5:1-11; 1 Corinthians 11:30-31; Hebrews 10:26-31.

"For me, passages like this are evidence of the supernatural origin and trustworthiness of the Bible. This Uzzah story goes so against the grain of human preferences. We would never have 'invented' a God like this — not if we want to win converts and influence people. This God is not very marketable. Anyone who says the God of the Bible is merely a projection of our wish fulfillment has not read the Bible."[3]

The Lord's wrath had broken out against Uzzah (6:8). "Anyone reading through 2 Samuel cannot help remembering how the same root was used four times in 5:20. . . . Yahweh 'breaks out' against David's enemies; in 6:8 against David's friend. Yahweh may break out against the Philistines — or against Israel. God's lethal holiness levels both pagans and churchmen. . . . The application of the text is clear: you dare not trifle with a God who is both real and holy."[4]

That place is called Perez Uzzah (6:8). Meaning "outbreak against Uzzah." In 5:20, Baal Perazim means "the lord who breaks out."

For Further Study:
Read Psalms 24,
47, 68, 99, and 132
to explore links in
phrasing and theme
to 2 Samuel 6. Taken
together with
2 Samuel 6, what are
the most important
attitudes and prin-
ciples that they teach
for the worship of
God?

5. What does Obed-Edom's experience in 6:11-12
   tell us about the ark and about God's ways and
   character?

   _____

   _____

   _____

Had taken six steps (6:13). This may well mean
   that sacrifices were offered not just after the
   first six steps, but continually—after every six
   steps along the way.

---

6. How would you characterize the overall tone of
   6:12-15, and what explanation would you give
   for it?

   _____

   _____

   _____

"Whether you can comprehend it or not,
2 Samuel 6 teaches that a fearful sense
of God's holiness does not suppress joy,
but stimulates it. Psalm 2:11 pulls it all
together in three words: 'Rejoice with
trembling!'"[5]

7. What is revealed about Saul's daughter Michal
   in 6:16-23?

   _____

   _____

   _____

   _____

116

It was before the LORD . . . I will celebrate before the LORD (6:21). "David makes it clear that he is very much concerned about how the Lord evaluates his actions."[6]

"Michal and David . . . represent two kingdoms. The old regime craves propriety, the new celebrates joy. Michal is like someone putting new wine into old wineskins — it simply doesn't work (Mark 2:18-22)."[7]

8. "Two threads of action make up the story of David's heroic life: the public life of a king and the personal life of a family man."[8] What is especially revealing about both of those story threads in 2 Samuel 6?

_____

_____

_____

_____

"Observe how 2 Samuel 6 portrays David in a priestly as well as a kingly role. He wears a linen ephod (verse 14), which seems to be a priestly garment (1 Samuel 2:18; 22:18), and he utters a blessing on the people (verse 18), a priestly function (Numbers 6:22-27). . . . We should not miss this glimpse of the king in a priestly role, for we will meet it again in prophecy (Psalm 110:1,4 and Zechariah 6:12-13), and yet again in person, in Jesus, David's Descendant, our reigning king and interceding priest."[9]

For Further Study:
How is the dramatic story of the ark — as presented in 1 Samuel 4–6 and here in 2 Samuel 6 — brought to completion in 1 Kings 8:1-9?

For Further Study:
The title for David's Psalm 30 includes the words "For the dedication of the temple." In its final form, it may have been revised by David for use after his death once the temple was finally dedicated by his son Solomon (see 1 Kings 8). In its original form, Psalm 30 may have reflected the events of 2 Samuel 6, which prefigured the building of the temple. In Psalm 30, how might verses 4-5 and 11-12 be reflective of the joyous day in 2 Samuel 6:12-15 when David brought the ark to Jerusalem?

Optional Application: What truths revealed in 2 Samuel 6 have a bearing on the way Christians are called to worship God today?

117

Optional Application: Look again at Nathan's words to David in 7:3: "Whatever you have in mind [literally, "all that is in your heart"], go ahead and do it, for the LORD is with you." In our own lives, when can we legitimately and confidently follow this same counsel?

For 2 Samuel 7, see the parallel account in 1 Chronicles 17.

The Great Promise (2 Samuel 7)

Nathan the prophet (7:2). He "appears here for the first time in the text. In addition to being the recipient of the divine oracle outlining the Davidic covenant (verses 4-17), Nathan confronts David after his sin with Bathsheba (chapter 12) and plays a prominent role in the anointing of Solomon (rather than Adonijah) as David's successor (1 Kings 1). He was also responsible for recording many of the events of the reigns of David (1 Chronicles 29:29) and Solomon (2 Chronicles 9:29)."[10]

9. What do you think was right and appropriate about David's desire to build a "house" for the Lord, as reflected in his words to Nathan in 7:2?

_____

_____

_____

10. In 7:3, when Nathan tells the king to go ahead and do "whatever you have in mind" (literally, "all that is in your heart"), what does this apparently include?

_____

_____

_____

"Nathan agrees that the king should do whatever he has 'in mind' (verse 3). The statement is that of a loyal subject following protocol (see 1 Samuel 14:7). . . .

Indeed, Nathan understands that David will ultimately follow the path of obedient servanthood (verse 5) because 'the Lord is with' him (verse 3; see verse 9; see also 5:10; 1 Samuel 16:18)."[11]

Optional Application: What specific assurance and confidence can we gain today from better understanding the biblical emphasis on God's concern for His people's safety? What does this emphasis mean personally for you? Express your gratitude for this in prayer to your Father in heaven.

11. In the Lord's words to David through Nathan in 7:4-17, what is revealed about God's ways of dealing with His people?

_____

_____

_____

12. According to what is spoken to David in 7:4-16, what exactly has God already done for David?

_____

_____

_____

Are you the one to build me a house to dwell in? (7:5). "The real issue is that both the initiative to build a temple and the choice of the person for the task must come from God and not from an individual king. . . . First, God has not commanded the building of a temple either to any of the past leaders or to David himself (verses 6-7). Second, the choice of the person is God's affair."[12]

---

13. Also in 7:4-16, what exactly does God promise to do in the future for David?

_____

_____

_____

For Further Study:
What more do you discover about God's concern for His people's safety in these prophetic passages: Jeremiah 23:6; 32:37; 33:16; Ezekiel 28:26; 34:25,27-28; Hosea 2:18; Micah 4:4; Zephaniah 3:13; Zechariah 14:11?

For Further Study:
What repeated commitment from God toward His people do you find in these passages, and what is its significance: Exodus 6:7; Leviticus 26:12; Deuteronomy 26:17-18; Jeremiah 7:23; 30:22; 31:1,33; 32:38; Ezekiel 34:30; 36:28; 37:23; Hosea 1:9-10; 2:23; Hebrews 8:10?

For Further Study:
How are God's words to David (through Nathan) in 7:8-16 reflected in David's later counsel to his son Solomon in 1 Kings 2:1-4?

I brought the Israelites up . . . to this day (7:6). "The irony . . . must not be missed: Although God condescends to accompany his people on their journey with a tent as his dwelling (verse 6b), a tent carried by them, all along they have in fact been carried by him (verse 6a)."[13] "I have been moving from place to place with a tent as my dwelling" (2 Samuel 7:6).

I will also give you rest from all your enemies (7:11). See also Deuteronomy 12:9-11 and 1 Kings 8:56. "Israel's security is at the center of Yahweh's concern. . . . Yahweh wants his people to have a home and to enjoy it in safety."[14]

"Although chapter 7 nowhere contains the word 'covenant,' it is universally recognized that it describes the Lord's covenant with David. Several Old Testament texts do in fact refer to Nathan's oracle as the exposition of a 'covenant' established by the Lord with his servant."[15] (See 2 Samuel 23:5; 1 Kings 8:23; 2 Chronicles 13:5; Psalm 89:3,28,34,39; 132:12; Isaiah 55:3; Jeremiah 33:21.)

14. What does the promise in verse 15 indicate to us about the nature of God's love?

_____

_____

_____

15. In what ways should we understand God's promises in 7:4-16 as pointing to Jesus Christ? How do they depend on Christ for their most complete fulfillment?

_____

_____

_____

16. How is the permanence of the promised "house" emphasized in 7:12-16?

_____

_____

"Not the least because they are cited twice in the New Testament (2 Corinthians 6:18; Hebrews 1:5), the Lord's words in verse 14a are doubtless the best known as well as the most solemn in the entire chapter: 'I [emphatic] will be his father, and he [emphatic] will be my son.' . . . Although the New Testament leaves no doubt that verse 14a is fulfilled typologically in Jesus, it is also clear that in its original setting the entire verse refers to the Lord's adoption of Solomon (and his royal descendants) as his son/vassal. . . . Such an understanding in no way denies the interpretation that Solomon, the type, prefigures Jesus."[16]

17. In 7:18-29, what do you see as the most significant aspects of David's response to God? What does he acknowledge in regard to what God has already done? What does David specifically praise God for? What does he specifically ask God for?

_____

_____

_____

"David's prayer does not begin with petition but with wonder, not with supplication but with surprise. He is

Optional Application: Look again closely at what the Lord tells David in 7:8-9. If the Lord sent a prophet to *you* with a statement expressing the essence of what God has already done for you, and what He promises to do for you in the future — what would that statement say?

For Further Study: David recognized the unique fact that God's people were redeemed (see 7:23). What should we keep in mind about this uniqueness, according to these passages: 1 Corinthians 6:19-20; Titus 2:14; 1 Peter 1:18-19?

Optional Application: How should Christians today view their uniqueness as redeemed people? And what does this mean personally for you?

breathless over Yahweh's grace and opens his prayer by staggering under it."[17]

This decree . . . is for a mere human! (7:19). Also translated, "this is instruction for mankind" (ESV). "A literal translation of the Hebrew text would be: 'And this the torah of man.' . . . David . . . seems to see that the kingship Yahweh guaranteed his dynasty would not only bring rest to Israel (verses 10-11) but would extend Yahweh's sway and benefits to all humanity—as if the Davidic dynasty were to be the mechanism for fulfilling the Abrahamic promise of blessing to 'all the families of the earth' (Genesis 12:3)."[18]

According to your will (7:21). Literally, "according to your heart." "Yahweh's kingdom plan arises solely out of Yahweh's choice and desire, not from any human ingenuity, least of all David's."[19]

There is no one like you (7:22). See this theme also in Hannah's praise in 1 Samuel 2:2.

The one nation on earth that God went out to redeem as a people for himself . . . whom you redeemed (7:23). "David knows that Israel is unique because she is a *redeemed* people."[20]

---

18. As David prays in 7:25-29, in what ways does he link his petition to God's promises?

_____

_____

_____

19. What does 7:21 reveal about David's understanding of God? In the full context of this prayer, what does David recognize about God's character and will? What does this verse reveal about David's faith in God and his expectations of God?

_____

_____

_____

Optional Application: From David's prayer in 7:18-29, what can we learn for strengthening our own faith in God and our confidence in His promises?

"The major lesson David teaches here [in 2 Samuel 7]: prayer pleads promises. Or, in David's own words, 'Do as you have promised' (verse 25). . . . That is at the heart of our praying. Yahweh's promise gives prayer its passion, boldness, and confidence."[21]

For Further Study: Looking ahead, read over David's charge to the people of Israel, and to Solomon his son, as recorded in 1 Chronicles 28:1-10 and 28:20. How do you see David's thoughts and instructions being influenced by his experience in 2 Samuel 7?

"Second Samuel 7 is a turning point in the history of salvation; it clearly advances the messianic hope in the Abrahamic covenant. True, Saul was also anointed by Yahweh. David in fact called Saul 'the Lord's anointed' (e.g., 1 Samuel 24:6) until the end. Yet God chose David, the youngest and forgotten son of Jesse, to establish a dynasty. David was used for God's eternal plan of salvation, not because he was perfect and ideal from a human viewpoint, but because the Lord was 'with him' and David found favor in God's sight."[22]

20. Notice how often the word *forever* is used in chapter 7. In each of the following verses, what is being highlighted by the use of this word?

7:13

_____

_____

_____

Optional Application: What is the application of 7:23-24 to the church today? What do these verses help teach us about how God wants us to understand our identity as *His* people?

For Further Study: Read over Psalm 89:19-37. How do you see this psalm reflecting and further amplifying God's covenant with David (plus David's response) in 2 Samuel 7, as well as David's anointing as king in 1 Samuel 16?

Optional Application: For Christians today, in what ways are the truths of 2 Samuel 7 related to our work as laborers in God's kingdom?

7:16 (twice)

_____

_____

_____

7:24

_____

_____

7:25

_____

_____

7:26

_____

_____

7:29 (twice)

_____

_____

_____

_____

"David . . . in spite of his moral failures, is God's choice to be the beginning of an enduring dynasty, from which the ultimate Ruler, who will lead Israel in bringing blessing to all the nations, will arise."[23]

David Victorious (2 Samuel 8)

For the following passages in 2 Samuel 8, see parallel accounts in 1 Chronicles as listed below:

- For verses 1-14, see 1 Chronicles 18:1-13 (see also 1 Kings 11:23-24).
- For verses 15-18, see 1 Chronicles 18:14-17.

21. What to you are the most impressive details mentioned in the record of David's victories in chapter 8?

_____

_____

_____

_____

22. What reason for David's victories is emphasized in 8:6 and 8:14, and what do you see as its full significance?

_____

_____

_____

_____

For Further Study: In 2 Samuel 7, God promises David a kingdom that would last forever. What more do these New Testament passages teach us about that everlasting kingdom? Matthew 5:3,10; 7:21; 13:24-52; 18:1-4; 24:14; 25:1-13; 25:34-40; Luke 1:33; 9:59-62; 12:29-32; 17:20-21; 22:29-30; John 18:36; Acts 14:22; Romans 14:17; 1 Corinthians 4:20; 15:50; Colossians 1:13-14; Hebrews 12:28; Revelation 1:5-6; 5:9-10; 11:15; 12:10-11.

Optional Application: In what ways do you see the kind of victories David experienced in 2 Samuel 8 as reflecting the life of spiritual victories that Christians are called to live today?

"Since David . . . is Yahweh's chosen, authorized king, David's kingdom is Yahweh's kingdom in (we might say) its introductory, visible form. Wherever David reigns, there the kingdom of God holds sway. . . . All this, however, is not David's achievement but Yahweh's gift, for 'Yahweh saved David wherever he went' (verses 6,14)."[24]

"David's kingdom is not a perfect but a preliminary and principal form of Christ's kingdom. The kingdom pattern, however, is the same: conflict precedes conquest. Both Old and New Testaments testify that, on the whole, men and nations do not long to receive but live to resist Christ's reign and that he will establish his rule at the last not by popular demand but by armed might. . . . That kingdom will come at the last because Christ, David's seed, imposes it over all objection and opposition and conquers all his and our enemies."[25]

23. What is important to note in the statement about David's rule in 8:15?

_____

_____

_____

_____

"Second Samuel 8 asserts that God's kingdom did come on earth under David's kingship, that the promise in 2 Samuel 7 did receive a real (though not final) fulfillment even in David's own time. . . . But the kingdom teaching of 2 Samuel 8 transcends the immediate historical situation — it describes what will always be true when God's kingdom is present and when it comes in its final form."[26]

David's Kindness (2 Samuel 9)

"David ... practiced covenant loyalty, and 2 Samuel 9 is the record of it."[27]

24. For the events in chapter 9, refer again to the background given in 2 Samuel 4:4. How would you summarize the major details in Mephibosheth's story, as presented so far?

_____

_____

_____

25. Notice the repeated mention in chapter 9 of Mephibosheth's being allowed to eat at David's table (in verses 7, 10, 11, and 13). How would you explain the significance of this?

_____

_____

_____

26. How would you compare the favor David shows to Mephibosheth (in chapter 9) with the favor God shows to us?

_____

_____

_____

"David's provision for Mephibosheth seems to have gone well beyond David's promise to Jonathan. . . . David doesn't merely spare Mephibosheth's life but heaps goodness on him. He not only protects his life but restores his inheritance. He not only saves him from

Optional Application: In your life, what are the most important ways that you're called to do what is "just and right" for everyone (as David did, according to 2 Samuel 8:15)?

Optional Application: What are the most important arenas of life in which you can demonstrate the kind of kindness that David demonstrates in 2 Samuel 9?

the shadow of death but prepares a table for him. David's kindness goes beyond survival to sustenance. Mephibosheth is cared for by and with the king and will never face destitution."[28]

Kindness (9:1,3,7). In all three instances, the Hebrew word is *hesed,* sometimes translated as "steadfast love" or "lovingkindness." This "is the devoted love promised within a covenant; *hesed* is love that is willing to commit itself to another by making its promise a matter of solemn record. So when David mentions *hesed* and 'for Jonathan's sake' we know he is alluding to the sacred commitment Jonathan had asked David to make in 1 Samuel 20:15."[29] (See also 1 Samuel 18:3; 20:8,16; 22:8; 23:18.)

"It takes no imagination but only faith to see that David's *hesed* is but a faithful reflection of Yahweh's — with whom there is no such thing as bare *hesed* (Psalm 23:1; John 1:16; 6:35; Romans 8:32)."[30]

Notice "a parallel between David's devoted love for his 'enemy' Mephibosheth — the sort of thing that wasn't supposed to happen — and something like Romans 5:10, 'While we were enemies we were reconciled to God.' . . . You will never appreciate David's covenant love unless you understand the source of it, the Author of it. In fact, is it not Paul's purpose in Romans 5:6-10 to highlight the who-could-have-guessed quality of God's love? Note his argument: 'While we were yet helpless . . . while we were yet sinners . . . while we were enemies' (verses 6,8,10). The first principle for grappling with the marvel of God's love is to realize that he has no business — in a sense — loving whom he loves. . . . We are the Lord's Mephibosheths, and there is absolutely no reason why we should be eating continually at the King's table."[31] And yet that is exactly what the Lord invites and calls us to continually do! (See, for example, John 14:23; Revelation 3:20.)

Optional Application: In what ways do you sense that your own relationship with the Lord is like Mephibosheth's relationship with King David?

Lesson Overview

27. In 2 Samuel 6–9, what confirmation do you see that David was truly a man after God's own heart (see 1 Samuel 13:14; Acts 13:22)? And what evidence here helps us understand what that description means?

_____

_____

_____

_____

28. What would you select as the key verse or passage in 2 Samuel 6–9 — one that best captures or reflects the dynamics of what these chapters are all about?

_____

_____

_____

_____

29. List any lingering questions you have about 2 Samuel 6–9.

_____

_____

_____

_____

For the Group

You may want to focus part of your discussion for lesson 7 on the following overall key themes from 2 Samuel. How do you see these themes developing in chapters 6–9? And what other recurring themes have you noticed?

- God's covenant with His people
- Godly leadership
- Sin, repentance, and forgiveness
- Community and family

The following numbered questions in lesson 7 may stimulate your best and most helpful discussion: 11, 13, 14, 15, 17, 18, 19, 22, 26, 27, 28, and 29.

Look also at the questions in the margin under the heading "For Thought and Discussion."

1. Dale Ralph Davis, *2 Samuel: Out of Every Adversity*, Focus on the Bible Commentary Series (Fearn, Scotland: Christian Focus, 1999), 73.
2. Davis, 75.
3. Davis, 75.
4. Davis, 77.
5. Davis, 78.
6. Ronald F. Youngblood, *Expositor's Bible Commentary,* ed. Frank E. Gaebelein, vol. 3, *1–2 Samuel* (Grand Rapids, MI: Zondervan, 1992), 877.
7. Davis, 79.
8. *ESV Study Bible* (Wheaton, IL: Crossway, 2008), introduction to 1–2 Samuel: "Literary Features."
9. Davis, 80.
10. Youngblood, 885.
11. Youngblood, 885.
12. Michiko Ita, "A Note on 2 Sam. 7," in *A Light unto My Path*, Gettysburg Theological Studies 4, ed. Howard N. Bream, Ralph D. Heim, and Carey A. Moore (Philadelphia: Temple University: 1974), 406, quoted in Youngblood, *1, 2 Samuel*, 886.
13. Youngblood, 887.
14. Davis, 90.
15. Youngblood, 881.
16. Youngblood, 893.
17. Davis, 98.
18. Davis, 100.
19. Davis, 100.
20. Davis, 102.

21. Davis, 105–106.
22. *ESV Study Bible*, introduction to 1–2 Samuel: "2 Samuel Key Themes."
23. *ESV Study Bible*, introduction to 1–2 Samuel: "History of Salvation Summary."
24. Davis, 111.
25. Davis, 112.
26. Davis, 109–110.
27. Davis, 119.
28. Davis, 124.
29. Davis, 120.
30. Davis, 124.
31. Davis, 126.

2 SAMUEL 10–14

A Turning Point of Sin

More Victories (2 Samuel 10)

> For 2 Samuel 10:1-19 see the parallel account in 1 Chronicles 19:1-19.

"Second Samuel 10 is but a miniature of Psalm 2 and proclaims: In spite of all resistance and hostility the David king will rule."[1]

1. Summarize the major developments narrated in chapter 10 regarding Israel's victories over Ammon and Syria.

_____

_____

_____

_____

_____

I will show kindness to Hanun . . . as his father showed kindness to me (10:2). The Hebrew word both times for "kindness" here is again *hesed*, the word for covenant-love.

For Further Study:
What specific parallels do you see between 2 Samuel 10 and Psalm 2?

133

For Thought and Discussion: In what ways does this chapter teach us about our need for the protection and grace of God?

2. a. What do you learn from chapter 10 about the leadership of Joab?

_____

_____

b. What significance do you see in Joab's words of encouragement to his troops in 10:12?

_____

_____

_____

c. What do you learn from this chapter about David's leadership?

_____

_____

_____

"Can we afford to allow this rascal Joab to preach truth to us? Could Joab be right? Should we listen to him?

"Why not? Why allow his unsavory character to eclipse the truth of his words? Can't even thugs speak truth?"[2]

David's Fall (2 Samuel 11)

> For 2 Samuel 11:1, see the parallel account in 1 Chronicles 20:1.

3. As the background to David's fall into sin with Bathsheba, what significant details are given in 11:1-4? What do these things reveal about David?

_____

_____

134

In chapter 11, the inner thoughts and feelings experienced by David, Bathsheba, Uriah, and Joab are not disclosed. "The writer seems to silence all feelings in order to isolate David's actions . . . to do all he can to keep the spotlight and the responsibility squarely on David."[3]

David sent Joab out with the king's men and the whole Israelite army (11:1). "The narrator thus leaves the impression that every able-bodied man in Israel goes to war—everyone, that is, except the king himself: 'But David remained in Jerusalem.' The contrast between David and his men could hardly be expressed in starker terms. Staying home in such situations was not David's usual practice, of course (see 5:2; 8:1-14; 10:17). Indeed, leading his troops into battle was expected to be the major external activity of an ancient Near Eastern ruler (see 1 Samuel 8:5-6,20). Although therefore reprehensible in itself, David's conduct on this occasion opens the way for the royal behavior that is more despicable still."[4]

She was purifying herself from her monthly uncleanness (11:4). The narrative shows irony: "Careful observance of the ceremonial law (Bathsheba's cleaning herself after her period) is followed by blatant transgression of the moral law (David's adultery with her)."[5]

"The warning in this text reaches far beyond King David and touches all professed servants of Christ. How suddenly and fatally any of us can fall! . . .

"Don't look at verses 1-5 and stammer something about your being a New Testament Christian. What difference

135

does that make? What immunity does that give you? If you begin to say, 'Oh, but I could never . . . ,' then you have already taken the first step in your fall. Don't ever be surprised at what you are capable of."[6]

4. Summarize the further developments in this situation as recorded in 11:5-13. What is revealed here about Uriah? What is revealed here about David?

_____

_____

_____

Go down to your house (11:8). Note how Uriah's refusal to do this is repeatedly emphasized in 11:8-13. More irony: "Uriah is disobedient (verse 9) to the king's order (verse 8), but the most moving faithfulness (verse 11) explains such disobedience."

Uriah said . . . (11:11). His only words in this chapter—"a speech expressing the acme of devotion and showing the reader that this Hittite is the only genuine Israelite in the whole chapter."[7]

To my wife (11:11). That Uriah "calls Bathsheba 'my wife' could hardly have failed to rebuke David, who had callously violated the relationship between Uriah and the person most precious to him."[8]

---

5. Summarize the further developments recorded in 11:14-27. What is revealed here about David?

_____

_____

_____

Yet more irony: "Joab's instructions to the messenger (verses 19-21) assume that King David has always been vigorously opposed to all unnecessary bloodshed in war. Joab's remarks reflect David's policy never to risk heedlessly the lives of one's men. Here, however, David finds a few lives needlessly snuffed out to be a piece of welcome news."[9]

David had her brought to his house (11:27). "David has persevered; he has succeeded. . . . Uriah the Hittite is dead. And David engineered it. He had arranged it all."[11]

The thing David had done displeased the LORD (11:27). More literally, "The thing David did was evil in the eyes of the LORD." "Not only had David brazenly violated God's laws but . . . he had shamelessly abused his royal power, which the Lord had entrusted to him to shepherd the Lord's people (5:2; 7:7-8)."[12]

For Further Study: Read Deuteronomy 27:24. Notice that David fell under the curse that is pronounced there. "The implication is obvious: David's heinous actions are punishable under the divine curse."[10] What punishment does David deserve?

Optional Application: What David did "displeased the LORD" (11:27) — it was evil in the Lord's sight. Is there an area in your life for which this statement would apply to your actions as well?

"The writer relates his whole sordid tale of lust and sex and deceit and murder without pausing to make marginal moral notations along the way. He details every step of the story as if God was nowhere involved. David was in control. This silence about God, however, only serves to accent the lone statement in verse 27b. It is as if David can vent his glands and weave his cover-up without any interference — until he runs smack into the judgment of God. It was evil in Yahweh's eyes. That's what Yahweh thought of it.

"The way the narrative is written, then, tells us that the silence of God does

137

Optional Application: In relation to your own sin, what are the most important truths that you see taught in 2 Samuel 11? What difference should it make in your life to embrace these truths more intensely?

For Further Study: Keeping in mind Nathan's story of the poor man's ewe lamb, look at brief parables in 1 Kings 20:35-43, Isaiah 5:1-7, and Jeremiah 3:1-5. How do they compare with the story Nathan told David?

For Thought and Discussion: Are all our sins truly "senseless" to the degree that David's sin with Bathsheba was? What do you think?

not indicate the absence of God. 'His eyes gaze upon, his eyelids test, the sons of men' (Psalm 11:4)."[13]

Confronted by God (2 Samuel 12)

6. If David and his actions were the dominating dynamic in chapter 11, what change in this regard do you see in chapter 12?

_____

_____

_____

7. How would you evaluate Nathan's approach in confronting David (see 12:1-7)?

_____

_____

_____

_____

The man . . . must die! (12:5). Literally, "the man is a son of death."

You are the man! (12:7). "What is both obvious and significant:" Nathan's statement to David "is the punchline not the introduction. . . . Nathan's strategy is nothing but the ingenuity of grace. His technique is the godly scheming of grace that goes around the end of our resistance and causes us to switch the floodlights on our own darkness. . . . Nathan's sword was within an inch of David's conscience before David knew that Nathan had a sword. That is the holy craftiness of grace."[14]

---

8. In 12:7-8, how does God communicate the senselessness of David's sin?

_____

_____

_____

9. Nathan said that David had "despised" both the Word of the Lord (see 12:9) and the Lord Himself (see 12:10). Why was this true in regard to David's actions?

_____

_____

_____

10. How would you characterize the manner in which the Lord chose to discipline David, as revealed in 12:10-14? What does this manner of discipline reveal about the Lord?

_____

_____

_____

Optional Application: When we sin, in what ways is this a *despising* of both God's Word and God Himself (as David was declared guilty of in 12:9-10)?

For Further Study: What punishment did David deserve for his sin, according to Leviticus 20:10 and Deuteronomy 22:22?

Optional Application: In light of how God dealt in chapter 12 with David's sins, what would you say is appropriate discipline from God for your own sins?

The sword . . . calamity . . . in broad daylight (12:10-12). "These verses are of major importance for the whole narrative; the reader will see how verses 10-12 control the rest of 2 Samuel."[15]

"To the extent that David understood that his role as human king was to implement the mandates of the Divine King, blessing would follow (see 2 Samuel 6:11-15,17-19; see especially 7:27-29). When he deliberately flouted God's will, however, he could count equally on the fact that he would be under the curse (see 12:1-18). And so it would be with his descendants on the throne:

Optional Application: What are some of the things for which you have honestly had to acknowledge (as David did in 12:13), "I have sinned against the LORD"?

For Further Study: The heading to Psalm 51 tells us that David wrote it at the time of the events in 2 Samuel 11–12. What are the most important ways in which Psalm 51 reveals and reflects David's circumstances and spiritual condition in 2 Samuel 11–12?

For Thought and Discussion: Since God had clearly indicated to David that Bathsheba's child would die because of David's sin (see 12:14), was it inappropriate for David to do what he does in 12:16? Why or why not?

If the Davidic covenant was eternal in the sense that his line would continue forever, it was also conditional in that individual participants in it would be punished when they sinned (see 1 Kings 2:4; 8:25; 9:4-5; Psalms 89:30-32; 132:12)."[16]

11. What things did God most want David to understand about his actions toward Bathsheba and Uriah, according to all the words spoken to David through the prophet Nathan in chapter 12?

_____

_____

_____

12. How would you explain the full meaning of David's words to Nathan in 12:13?

_____

_____

_____

13. What do the events in 12:15-25 reveal most clearly about David? What do the events in these verses reveal most about the Lord?

_____

_____

_____

14. How would you contrast David's response to a prophet's personal rebuke in 2 Samuel 12 with Saul's response to a prophet's personal rebuke in 1 Samuel 15?

_____

_____

_____

15. In 12:16-23, what do David's actions and words reveal about his understanding of God?

_____

_____

_____

The LORD may be gracious to me (12:22). "See how well David knows his God! Showing grace is Yahweh's forte. And who can tell what a God like that may delight to do in this case? Who can imagine how gracious a God of all grace wants to be to us in our sins and messes? For David, grace is not a doctrinal concept but the peculiar bent of God's nature."[17]

---

16. What does chapter 12 teach us about the grace of God?

_____

_____

_____

For 2 Samuel 12:29-31, see the parallel account in 1 Chronicles 20:1-3.

---

17. a. In 12:26-31, what do we learn about the military leadership of Joab?

_____

_____

b. What do we learn from these verses about David's leadership?

_____

_____

_____

Optional Application: In the future, in order to avoid sins like those David was confronted with in 2 Samuel 12, what particular help do you need from the Lord? Ask Him for that help, and record your prayer in writing.

Optional Application: For your own life, what are the most important truths about God's grace and fatherly discipline that you see taught in 2 Samuel 11? What difference should it make in your life to embrace these truths more intensely?

"Just because David is Yahweh's beloved and chosen king does not mean he retains the kingdom by any merit but only by grace, for he is a 'son of death' [see 12:5]. In 1–2 Samuel *all* human leadership is flawed, which means that the kingdom — if there is to be one — can be established and maintained only by grace. Hence 1–2 Samuel makes us lift our eyes to wait for the Messianic King."[18]

Family Disaster (2 Samuel 13–14)

18. a. Summarize the circumstances and events leading up to Amnon's sin, as narrated in 13:1-14.

    _____

    _____

    _____

   b. In the aftermath of Amnon's sin, what significant details are brought out in 13:15-22?

    _____

    _____

    _____

19. From 13:12 and 13:16, summarize the content of the protests made by Tamar in response to Amnon and indicate their significance.

    _____

    _____

    _____

    _____

    _____

"Readers will sense their sympathy welling up for Tamar, especially when they hear her two desperate pleas. Looking back over the story, we see her trapped (verses 5-11), ignored (14,16), raped (14), despised (15), banished (17), and ruined (18-20). We must do what Amnon did not do: listen to Tamar. The writer's viewpoint comes through Tamar's pleas, and we must hear her if we are to form a proper estimate of Amnon's deed."[19]

For Further Study:
"Rape was shameful enough; but this was more than rape. It was incest and was explicitly forbidden in the covenant law."[20] What do the following passages indicate about incest: Leviticus 18:9-11; 20:17; Deuteronomy 27:22?

20. Notice what is said about David in 13:21. In response to the abuse of his daughter Tamar and the sin of his son Amnon, no action from David is recorded. What might this reveal about David?

_____

_____

_____

_____

21. Summarize how Absalom got his revenge, as narrated in 13:23-29.

_____

_____

_____

22. From 13:30-39, describe the significant details in David's response to Absalom's actions.

_____

_____

_____

_____

For Further Study:
Compare your impressions of Absalom in these chapters with what the New Testament says about all of us (before we're reborn in Christ) in Titus 3:3. In what ways are all of us like Absalom? And what is our only hope, according to Titus 3:4?

"There was something right about David's fury. It should have led to a righteous result. His anger should have led to justice. Amnon should have been punished and Tamar exonerated."[21]

23. Give a brief summary description of the character and personality of each of these persons as revealed in 2 Samuel 13:

Amnon:

_____

_____

_____

Jonadab:

_____

_____

Tamar:

_____

_____

Absalom:

_____

_____

_____

David:

_____

_____

24. "All the way through 2 Samuel 13 . . . disaster follows disaster, and life in David's kingdom rushes along, driven by lust, conniving, weakness, and hatred. A shattered woman remains ignored by justice and unrestored by murder.

And God is never mentioned in the whole affair. What is Yahweh doing in all this?"[22] How would you answer that question?

_____

_____

_____

25. From the description in chapter 14 leading up to Absalom's being restored to David's presence, summarize . . .

Joab's actions and their consequences:

_____

_____

_____

Absalom's actions and their consequences:

_____

_____

_____

26. What differences do you see in the way that Nathan used a story to confront David in chapter 12 and the way that the woman of Tekoa used a story in confronting David in chapter 14?

_____

_____

_____

_____

27. What is noteworthy about the description of Absalom given in 14:25-27?

_____

_____

_____

"Physical presence before men without internal submission to God makes for leadership disaster."[23]

The king kissed Absalom (14:33). "David's kiss signifies Absalom's restoration to royal favor."[24]

Lesson Overview

28. In 2 Samuel 10–14, what confirmation do you see that David was a man after God's own heart (see 1 Samuel 13:14; Acts 13:22)? And what evidence here helps us understand what that description means?

_____

_____

_____

_____

29. What would you select as the key verse or passage in 2 Samuel 10–14 — one that best captures or reflects the dynamics of what these chapters are all about?

_____

_____

_____

_____

30. List any lingering questions you have about 2 Samuel 10–14.

_____

_____

_____

_____

146

For the Group

You may want to focus part of your discussion for lesson 8 on the following overall key themes from 2 Samuel. How do you see these themes developing in chapters 10–14? And what other recurring themes have you noticed?

- God's covenant with His people
- Godly leadership
- Sin, repentance, and forgiveness
- Community and family

The following numbered questions in lesson 8 may stimulate your best and most helpful discussion: 3, 8, 9, 10, 11, 12, 13, 15, 16, 23, 28, 29, and 30.

Remember to look also at the "For Thought and Discussion" questions in the margin.

1. Dale Ralph Davis, *2 Samuel: Out of Every Adversity*, Focus on the Bible Commentary Series (Fearn, Scotland: Christian Focus, 1999), 133.
2. Davis, 136.
3. Davis, 140–141.
4. Ronald F. Youngblood, *Expositor's Bible Commentary*, ed. Frank E. Gaebelein, vol. 3, *1–2 Samuel* (Grand Rapids, MI: Zondervan, 1992), 928.
5. Davis, 140–141.
6. Davis, 142–143.
7. Davis, 140.
8. Youngblood, 934.
9. Davis, 141.
10. Youngblood, 935.
11. Davis, 144.
12. *NIV Study Bible* (Grand Rapids, MI: Zondervan, 1985), on 2 Samuel 11:27.
13. Davis, 146.
14. Davis, 151–152, with Davis's acknowledgment of Alexander Whyte, *Bible Characters* (repr., Grand Rapids. MI: Zondervan, 1967), 1:245.
15. Davis, 152.
16. Youngblood, 562.
17. Davis, 158.
18. Davis, 160.
19. Davis, 164.
20. Davis, 165.
21. Davis, 170.
22. Davis, 173.
23. Davis, 184.
24. Davis, 181.

2 SAMUEL 15–20

Rebellions

A Son's Conspiracy (2 Samuel 15–17)

1. How would you summarize Absalom's actions
   and their consequences as revealed in 15:1-12?

   _____

   _____

   _____

He stole the hearts of the people of Israel (15:6).
   "This idiom . . . does not refer to capturing the
   affections but to duping the mind."[1]

2. How would you characterize David's response to
   hardship and crisis as revealed in 15:13-37?

   _____

   _____

   _____

*Wherever my lord the king may be, whether
   it means life or death, there will your servant be* (15:21). "Ittai is an island of fidelity in
   a sea of treachery. The irony is clear: David's
   own son, 'whom he loaded with undeserved
   kindness, was conspiring against him, while
   this stranger, who owed him nothing in

**Optional
Application:** In what
ways in your own life
can you identify with
David's dependence
on God's grace as
expressed, for his par-
ticular situation,
in 15:25?

comparison, was risking everything in his
cause.' . . . Here is Ittai, the foreigner, who
sticks closer than a brother (Proverbs 18:24),
and who, with his men and all their children,
tramps off after David to share his deliverance
or his doom."[2]

3. What is significant about David's sending the
   ark back into Jerusalem in 15:24-26?

   _____

   _____

   _____

   _____

If I find favor in the LORD's eyes (15:25). "Liberty
leaps out of those words. David . . . will not
repeat the fiasco of 1 Samuel 4:3. David says
his restoration (should there be such) does not
depend on whether he has Yahweh's furniture
[the ark] but on whether he has Yahweh's favor.
All rests on grace (verse 25). He submits to
Yahweh's sovereign sway. . . . This is not weak
resignation but robust submission. Here is the
freedom of faith in the will of God."[3]

4. a. What specific actions does David take in
      chapter 15 to undermine Absalom's rebellion?

      _____

      _____

      _____

   b. How do David's words and actions demon-
      strate his faith in God?

      _____

      _____

      _____

5. Summarize Ziba's actions and David's response as seen in 16:1-4. (We'll learn more about Ziba in chapter 19.)

_____

_____

_____

"For all the hints of faith it is still a dark day in Israel. Admittedly, David is suffering for his sins (12:10-12), but he is nevertheless the rightful king. But the rightful king has been rejected and plods up the Mount of Olives weeping (15:30). The scene will be repeated. The Descendant of David, the rightful king according to 7:12-16, will be seen on the Mount of Olives (Luke 19:37), and he will be weeping (Luke 19:41-44) not so much over his rejection as over the doom of those who have rejected him."[4]

6. From 16:5-14, summarize Shimei's actions, and the responses of both Abishai and David.

_____

_____

_____

7. How would you summarize Absalom's actions and his circumstances as presented in 16:15-23?

_____

_____

_____

Ahithophel answered, "Sleep with your father's concubines" (16:21). "Ahithophel is the Judas Iscariot of the Old Testament. . . . Ahithophel's advice that is meant to overthrow David's kingdom nevertheless carries out Yahweh's judgment upon David's sin [see 2 Samuel 12:11-12]. . . . That is why there is hope for God's people in this text, even though it depicts a judgment upon the covenant king, for the text is saying that the betrayer is yet in the hand of God. His act of treachery only executes God's word."[5]

He slept with his father's concubines (16:22). By this action, "Absalom told all Israel he was burning his bridges behind him; there was no turning back; he meant business; he had no intent or hope of reconciliation with David."[6] Refer also to 2 Samuel 12:11-12.

"David is not just anybody; . . . David must not be viewed as an individual but in terms of his office, in his vocation as Yahweh's covenant king. . . . This is not to deny David's sinfulness or the judgment he now suffers (even via Absalom). David is both under Yahweh's election and under Yahweh's judgment and yet remains Yahweh's appointed servant. And to despise, oppose, and betray him is to despise, oppose, and betray the God who appointed him."[7]

8. In chapter 17, how did God answer David's prayer of 15:31?

_____

_____

_____

_____

"When Bible readers come to 2 Samuel 17 they must keep their fingers on the promise of 1 Samuel 28:17, of 2 Samuel 3:18, 5:2, and 7:12-16. The right perspective is crucial. One must not focus on character studies or personal tragedies here; the chapter reports a threat to the kingdom of God and to God's anointed king. . . . 2 Samuel 17 . . . simultaneously shows Yahweh's kingdom under attack *and* the consolations his people still have in such times."[8]

9. From 16:16-19 and chapter 17, summarize Hushai's actions and their consequences.

_____

_____

_____

10. What are the specifics of the plan that Ahithophel proposed to Absalom in 17:1-4?

_____

_____

_____

11. a. What techniques and approaches does Hushai use to undermine Ahithophel's counsel in 17:7-13? In particular, how does he appeal to logic, to caution, and to Absalom's vanity?

_____

_____

_____

_____

For Further Study:
The heading to
Psalm 3 tells us that
David wrote it at the
time of the events
in 2 Samuel 15–17.
What are the most
important ways in
which Psalm 3 reveals
and reflects David's
circumstances and
spiritual condition in
2 Samuel 15–17?

b. What are the major ways that Hushai's plan
(see 17:7-13) differs from Ahithophel's (see
17:1-4)?

_____

_____

_____

Absalom said, "Summon also Hushai" (17:5).
"Why did he do it? Why did Absalom make that
fateful inquiry in verses 5-6? Why that first step
in his slide into the pit? . . . And he stupidly
handed Hushai a tremendous advantage. He
did not simply ask Hushai what should be done
in the present situation, but he divulged to him
Ahithophel's whole plan (verse 6) and asked for
his opinion, review, and comment. In this way
Hushai knew exactly what he was up against
and what his agenda must be."[9]

12. What do you see as the significance in the
statement in 17:14 about what the Lord was
determined to do?

_____

_____

_____

The LORD had determined (17:14). "That is the
explanation for the whole story—for all this
which has occurred so naturally, so humanly,
so freely. Yahweh had ordained it. That may
raise some questions for you. But remember:
Yahweh's sovereignty is not meant to give you
philosophical problems but spiritual comfort."[10]

The good advice of Ahithophel (17:14). Good "in
practical not moral terms, i.e., it was good
in the sense that it would have worked, been
effective."[11]

13. a. From 17:15-22, summarize how Hushai's news reached David and David's response.

   _____

   _____

   _____

   b. In 17:23, how did Ahithophel respond to the turn of events, and why do you think he responded in this way?

   _____

   _____

   _____

14. How would you summarize David's actions and his circumstances as portrayed in 17:24-29?

   _____

   _____

   _____

For Further Study:
Also compare 2 Samuel 15–17 with the situation described in the heading or title to Psalm 63. In what ways does the content of Psalm 63 seem to reflect David's circumstances and spiritual condition in these chapters in 2 Samuel?

For Further Study:
What similarities do you see between the story of Absalom in chapters 15–18 and the later story of his brother Adonijah in 1 Kings 1:5–2:25?

Confronting the Rebellion

(2 Samuel 18–19)

15. From 18:1-18, summarize the events leading up to Absalom's death and burial.

   _____

   _____

   _____

Threw him into a big pit . . . and piled up a large heap of rocks over him (18:17). "This is the burial of an accursed man."[12] See the similar burials in Joshua 7:26, 8:29, and 10:27. (See also Deuteronomy 21:23.)

I have no son (18:18). The sons of Absalom mentioned earlier (in 14:27) must have died before Absalom did.

"We must see that Absalom's end is a microcosm. His death as a man under the curse is typical of what will be the lot of all who at any time set themselves against God's kingdom, his chosen King, and/or his people. This is a somber truth, but Yahweh's true subjects have no hope unless it *is* true."[13]

16. From 18:16-33, contrast the responses of Joab and David to the fact of Absalom's death.

_____

_____

_____

_____

17. How are David and Joab contrasted in chapter 19?

_____

_____

_____

_____

Weeping and mourning (19:1). "I suggest there is a deeper dimension to David's grief. . . . We must allow 12:10-12 to illumine David's sorrow. How Nathan's words in this latter text must have echoed in David's conscience. 'The sword will not depart from your house forever' (12:10). It is David's guilt that inflames his grief. . . . David knew that his sin had set the sword loose in his household. 'If only I had died instead of you!' [18:33]. David was the guilty one yet Absalom suffers the consequences of David's guilt. (This does not negate Absalom's own guilt.)"[14]

18. How would you summarize the confrontation between Joab and David in 19:1-8?

_____

_____

_____

"Joab is an enigma. Here in 19:1-8 Joab seems to be right, yet in 18:14-15 he is insubordinate. Joab was wrong to defy the king's order, yet he clearly divined what disaster David's incessant grief would bring. Thus Joab is wrong and right; he is rebellious and reasonable. He lacks subordination but not sense. . . .

"The writer may sympathize with David's condition but he agrees with Joab's mind. Hence Joab's speech [see 19:5-7] is nasty but necessary."[15]

19. Summarize the developments in David's situation and circumstances as narrated in 19:8-15.

_____

_____

_____

_____

20. In 19:16-23, how would you summarize David's treatment of Shimei (for background, review 16:5-13)?

_____

_____

_____

_____

21. a. Looking ahead, what will David later counsel his son Solomon—Israel's next king—to do with regard to Shimei (see 1 Kings 2:8-9)?

_____

_____

_____

b. What further events will bring a final close to Shimei's story in 1 Kings 2:36-46?

_____

_____

_____

22. In 19:24-30, how would you summarize David's treatment of Mephibosheth and Ziba (for background, refer to 4:4; 9:1-13; 16:1-4)?

_____

_____

_____

_____

23. a. In 19:31-39, how would you summarize David's treatment of Barzillai (for background, refer to 17:27-29)?

_____

_____

_____

_____

b. Looking ahead, what will David later counsel Solomon to do with regard to Barzillai's family (see 1 Kings 2:7)?

_____

_____

_____

Let your servant return, that I may die in my own town (19:37). "Barzillai's farewell request does breathe an air of contentment (not simply resignation). He was eighty years old when he performed what was arguably his most important service for the kingdom of God. Barzillai had been faithful to Yahweh's covenant king. Besides that, what else matters? What ever could one want beyond that? A man like that is free—content to go back to his hometown and finish out his days."[16]

24. From 19:40-43, explain the tension that arose between Judah and the other tribes of Israel, and the reasons for it.

_____

_____

_____

_____

Further Rebellion (2 Samuel 20)

"As we read through the chapter we know we have heard this before. There are no surprises—only more rebellion, more tragedy."[17]

25. How would you explain the nature and cause of Sheba's rebellion as seen in chapter 20?

_____

_____

_____

26. What is the significance of David's actions in 20:3, in light of what we saw earlier in 12:11-12, 15:16, and 16:20-22?

_____

_____

_____

_____

***They were kept in confinement till the day of
their death, living as widows*** (20:3). "There
is something intensely, irretrievably sad about
verse 3."[18]

---

27. Compare Joab's attack against Amasa in
20:8-10 with his slayings of Abner (see 3:26-27)
and Absalom (see 18:14-15). Together, what do
these incidents seem to tell us about Joab?

_____

_____

_____

***Over Israel's entire army . . . in charge of forced
labor . . . recorder . . . secretary . . . priests***
(20:23-26). "In their own way, these verses
quietly say that the kingdom of David is still
intact. The kingdom is fragile because of the
sinfulness of the king and because of the rebel-
lions of Absalom and Sheba. Yet in spite of all
the corruption from within and attacks from
without, the kingdom is still standing. Its
administrators are all at work."[19]

Lesson Overview

28. In 2 Samuel 15–20, what confirmation do you
see that David was a man after God's own heart
(see 1 Samuel 13:14; Acts 13:22)? And what
evidence here helps us understand what that
description means?

_____

_____

_____

29. What would you select as the key verse or passage in 2 Samuel 15–20 — one that best captures or reflects the dynamics of what these
chapters are all about?

_____

_____

_____

30. List any lingering questions you have about
2 Samuel 15–20.

_____

_____

_____

_____

For the Group

You may want to focus part of your discussion for
lesson 9 on the following overall key themes from
2 Samuel. How do you see these themes developing in chapters 15–20? And what other recurring
themes have you noticed?

- God's covenant with His people
- Godly leadership
- Sin, repentance, and forgiveness
- Community and family

The following numbered questions in lesson 9
may stimulate your best and most helpful discussion: 2, 8, 12, 26, 28, 29, and 30.
Remember to look also at the "For Thought and
Discussion" questions in the margin.

1. Dale Ralph Davis, *2 Samuel: Out of Every Adversity*, Focus on the Bible Commentary Series (Fearn, Scotland: Christian Focus, 1999), 189.
2. Davis, 192, quoted in W. G. Blaikie, "The Second Book of Samuel," *The Expositor's Bible* (Cincinnati: Jennings & Graham, n.d.), 232.
3. Davis, 194.
4. Davis, 197.
5. Davis, 206, 208.
6. Davis, 207.
7. Davis, 200.
8. Davis, 211.
9. Davis, 212.
10. Davis, 214.
11. Davis, 214.
12. P. Kyle McCarter, "II Samuel," *The Anchor Bible* (New York: Doubleday, 1984), 407, quoted in Davis, 227.
13. Davis, 228.
14. Davis, 235–236.
15. Davis, 231.
16. Davis, 247.
17. Davis, 249.
18. Davis, 250.
19. Davis, 258.

2 SAMUEL 21–24

Deliverance Remembered

"These chapters are . . . the intended wrap-up for all 1–2 Samuel; in them the writer wants to show us how we are to regard God's kingdom as it is ordered under David.

"Though these chapters are sometimes viewed as a collection of fragments, it has long been recognized that they are a carefully organized collection of fragments. The six sections have been arranged in an obviously deliberate structure (which ought to suggest, by the way, that the writer had a definite purpose in mind in including them)."[1]

Vengeance (2 Samuel 21:1-15)

During the reign of David (21:1). "By this very general time reference the writer keeps us from assuming that the episode of 21:1-14 followed chronologically the events of 2 Samuel 20."[2]

Famine (21:1). See Leviticus 26:19-20.

On account of Saul and his blood-stained house; it is because he put the Gibeonites to death (21:1). See 1 Samuel 22:16-19; Joshua 9:15,19; Numbers 35:33.

1. In 21:1-14, what does David seek to accomplish in regard to the Gibeonites, and for what reason?

_____

_____

_____

Given to us to be killed and their bodies exposed before the LORD (21:6). "God's wrath . . . stands behind Gibeon's request. Yahweh has already mercifully signaled this in the famine (verse 1). Yahweh's wrath then must be appeased, satisfied, or—to use the old word—propitiated. The curse of the covenant must be carried out."[3]

2. What is significant about David's decision regarding Mephibosheth in 21:7?

_____

_____

_____

3. What significance do you see in the actions of Rizpah in 21:10?

_____

_____

_____

"Here is heart-and-gut-wrenching misery. And the writer would fill your senses with it. As if to say: Look what comes from covenant-breaking."[4]

God answered prayer in behalf of the land (21:14). "God approved—or at least accepted—the measures taken to turn away his wrath for covenant-breaking. Now Israel could move from famine to favor."[5]

Optional Application: From 2 Samuel 21:1-14, what new appreciation do you gain personally of the atonement for your sins that Christ accomplished on the cross?

"Most readers . . . are simply aghast at the sheer horror of the episode [in 21:1-14]. That, I suggest, points us to its primary application. Readers should be aghast. The text says atonement *is* horrible, it *is* gory. Atonement is never nice but always gruesome. We need to see this for we easily fall into the trap of regarding atonement as merely a doctrine, a concept, an abstraction to be explained, a bit of theology to be analyzed. . . . But we should know better. . . . From slicing the bull's throat in Leviticus 1 all the way to Calvary, God has always said atonement is nasty and repulsive. Christians must beware of becoming too refined, longing for a kinder, gentler faith. If we've grown too used to Golgotha, perhaps Gibeah (verse 6) can shock us back into truth: atonement is a drippy, bloody, smelly business. The stench of death hangs heavy wherever the wrath of God has been quenched."[6]

Heroes in Battle (2 Samuel 21:15-22)

For 2 Samuel 21:18-22, see the parallel account in 1 Chronicles 20:4-8.

For Further Study:
David says that God "soared on the wings of the wind" (22:11). How do you also see God associated with storm winds in Psalm 104:3, Isaiah 29:6, Ezekiel 13:13, and Nahum 1:3?

4. a. In 21:15-22, what details stand out most to you in the accounts of these battles?

_____

_____

_____

b. How does this section point to the fulfillment of 2 Samuel 3:18?

_____

_____

_____

The lamp of Israel (21:17). Decades later, in 1 Kings 11:36, God promises that David will "always have a lamp before me in Jerusalem." (This "lamp" is mentioned again in 1 Kings 15:4 and 2 Kings 8:19.) "The Davidic flame will always burn."[7] A lamp in Scripture often represents something living (such as a person's life—see, for example, Job 18:6), and the extinguishing of that lamp represents its death. In Psalm 132:17, God makes this promise: "Here I will make a horn grow for David and set up a lamp for my anointed one."

He taunted Israel (21:21). This same Hebrew verb is used repeatedly of Goliath's words. See 1 Samuel 17:10,25-26,36,45.

David's song in 2 Samuel 22 is also recorded, with slight revisions, in Psalm 18.

A Song of Deliverance (2 Samuel 22)

5. a. How would you describe the level of intensity in David's praise for God in 22:1-4? What specific reasons for that intensity does David give in 22:5-20?

_____

_____

_____

b. What is revealed about God and His character in 22:8-20?

_____

_____

_____

For Further Study: Read over Leviticus 26 and Deuteronomy 28 in light of David's words in 2 Samuel 22. How do those earlier passages indicate positive reward for those who obey the Lord's Word and negative consequences for those who don't?

> Instead of the long description of God's actions we see in 22:8-16, "David . . . could simply have written, 'Yahweh intervened on my behalf.' Why didn't he? . . . David doesn't merely want to tell you a fact about Yahweh, he wants you to see Yahweh in all his saving fury. He doesn't intend merely to inform you about what God has done; he wants you to see the God who did it."[8]

Optional Application: What is it in the gospel of Christ that makes it possible for you to say with David (in 22:25), "The LORD has rewarded me according to my righteousness, according to my cleanness in his sight"?

6. a. Summarize what David is saying about himself and about God in 22:21-28.

_____

_____

_____

Optional Application: What truths in David's song in 2 Samuel 22 do you personally want most to praise God for and to thank Him for?

b. What are we meant to comprehend about God's power from what David says in 22:29-31?

_____

_____

_____

Blameless before him (22:24). The Hebrew for "blameless" used here "does not connote sinlessness but wholeness, completeness,

For Further Study:
Look at Judges 10:6-14, Psalm 50:16-23, and Jeremiah 2:26-29. These passages paint the picture of what David's life would have been like if he had not been consistently committed to the Lord. How would you describe that picture?

Optional Application: To live your life in a way that rightly reflects the truths David sings about in 2 Samuel 22, what particular help do you need from the Lord? Ask Him for that help, and record your prayer in writing.

integrity. David does not claim perfection in life's particulars but wholeheartedness in life's commitment." Likewise, "when David speaks of his righteousness and purity (verses 21,25) he does not point to sinless perfection but life direction; he is not sporting a pharisaical pride over errorless obedience but expressing a faithful loyalty via consistent obedience."[9]

7. What specific actions by God on David's behalf does he highlight in 22:32-49?

_____

_____

_____

You armed me with strength . . . you humbled my adversaries before me. You made my enemies turn their backs (22:40-41). "David is crystal clear. All that he has been able to do has been done by Yahweh's power. . . . David's kingdom rests on Yahweh's muscle."

A Last Statement (2 Samuel 23:1-7)

Last words of David (23:1). "Probably to be understood as David's last poetic testimony (in the manner of his psalms), perhaps composed at the time of his final instructions and warnings to his son Solomon (see 1 Kings 2:1-10)."[10]

8. a. What does David emphasize about God in 23:1-7?

_____

_____

_____

b. In what ways do the words of 23:3-4 point to Christ?

_____

_____

_____

"David . . . knows that the hope of the future ruler (verses 3-4) is simply the fulfillment of the 'everlasting covenant' Yahweh had already instigated with him (7:12-16), 'a covenant fully stated and secured.' . . . A righteous Ruler over mankind is coming to reign."[11]

Like the light of morning at sunrise on a cloudless morning, like the brightness after rain that brings grass from the earth (23:4). "The kingdom is attractive because the King is attractive. And the King is attractive because we have seen so little of this kind of ruler. Where, from democracy to dictatorship, have we found a ruler so controlled by godly fear and personal righteousness that his tenure actually revives and renews his people?"[12]

Mighty Men (2 Samuel 23:8-39)

For 2 Samuel 23:8-39, see the parallel account in 1 Chronicles 11:11-41.

9. In 23:8-39, what particular exploits of these mighty men are most impressive to you?

_____

_____

_____

For Further Study: How would you compare these "last words of David" in chapter 23 with the blessings given before their deaths by Isaac (see Genesis 27:2-4,26-29), Jacob (see Genesis 49), and Moses (see Deuteronomy 33)?

Optional Application: What will your life look like for *you* to be able to say joyfully and gratefully with David (in 22:33), "It is God who arms me with strength and keeps my way secure"?

For Further Study: In 2 Samuel 23:7, David speaks of how evil men are "burned up where they lie." How is this fact of eternal destiny confirmed by Jesus in these passages: Matthew 13:41-42; 25:41; Mark 9:43-49; Luke 16:23-24? (See also Revelation 21:8,27; 22:15.)

For Thought and Discussion: How important is it to maintain a sense of mystery in our perspective on God?

"Behind all such daring courage and dogged combat stands the fact that the victory was Yahweh's gift. He used courage and gall to bring his 'great salvation,' but in the last analysis the deliverance was his doing. All God's servants must recognize this secret lest we fail to see our successes as gifts and turn them — or ourselves — into idols."[13]

Thirty chief warriors . . . the Thirty (23:13,23-24). "The 'Thirty' probably serves more as a general category than a precise figure. Over time some would fall in battle (e.g., Asahel, verse 24; see 2 Samuel 2:18-23) and others would be added. But their names are here — each of them one of David's most esteemed and loyal troops. Their names are here because they excelled in their calling — fighting for David's kingdom."[14]

Uriah the Hittite (23:39). "One name, the last in the list of 'The Thirty,' punches our replay button and we see and hear the whole mess again. Is there no escape? Not in 2 Samuel. . . . It's as if the writer had smeared bright yellow highlighting across Uriah's name. No reader can fail to remember."[15]

Sin, Judgment, and Atonement

(2 Samuel 24)

> For 2 Samuel 24, see the parallel account in 1 Chronicles 21.

10. In 24:1-9, what did David command Joab to do, and what were the results?

170

_____

_____

"Second Samuel 24 does not explicitly tell us why the census was wrong. . . . It was wrong but we needn't know why. . . .

"Yahweh's wrath burns against Israel and he is going to use David's sin as the vehicle of his wrath upon Israel. But why is Yahweh angry against Israel? We do not know. We are not told. . . .

"Does this bother us? Do we perhaps assume that God must always explain himself and justify his ways? If we cannot be content to accept the mystery of this text we may be revealing ourselves. If we are upset over a text that tells us Yahweh is angry but does not tell us why, are we not saying that we really don't trust him to be just?"[16]

Why does my lord the king want to do such a thing? (24:3). "If the census bothered Joab, there must have been something terribly amuck with it; Joab was not famous for a tender conscience."[17]

---

11. In 24:10, what did David realize and acknowledge before God?

_____

_____

_____

12. In 24:11-15, what options were offered to David, and what was the result of David's choice?

13. a. What significance do you see in David's words about God in 24:14?

b. How did David know this to be true about God? (See also 12:22 and 16:12.)

His mercy is great (24:14). "David is about to meet Yahweh's wrath and yet is convinced of Yahweh's mercies. Somehow he imagines that the hand that strikes him will nevertheless spare him. David's assumptions are astounding! His words in verse 14 breathe not only necessary resignation but boundless consolation. See how well he knows his God!"[18]

> David said to Gad, "I am in deep distress. Let us fall into the hands of the LORD, for his mercy is great; but do not let me fall into human hands" (2 Samuel 24:14).

14. What cause for ending the pestilence is indicated in 24:16?

15. What does 24:17 indicate about David's heart?

_____

_____

_____

16. What did the Lord command David to do in 24:18-19?

_____

_____

_____

17. How does 24:25 relate to 24:16?

_____

_____

_____

The LORD answered his prayer in behalf of the land (24:25). Recall also the same phrasing in 21:14.

_____

18. What do we learn about God in chapter 24, especially in regard to His wrath and His mercy?

_____

_____

_____

_____

Lesson Overview

19. Recall once again Scripture's emphasis that David was a man after God's own heart (see 1 Samuel 13:14; Acts 13:22). What confirmation of that fact do you see in these final four chapters of 2 Samuel? And what evidence here helps us understand what that description means?

For Further Study:
"David built an altar" (24:25) at a site where the altar of the temple would later stand. In Hebrews 13:10, Christians are told that we, too, have an altar. What is our altar, as believers in Christ? (See also 1 Corinthians 5:7 and Revelation 5:9,12.)

Optional Application: Which verses in 1 and 2 Samuel would be most helpful for you to memorize, so you have them always available in your mind and heart for the Holy Spirit to use?

173

_____

_____

_____

_____

20. What would you select as the key verse or passage in 2 Samuel 21–24—one that best captures or reflects the dynamics of what these chapters are all about?

_____

_____

_____

_____

21. List any lingering questions you have about 2 Samuel 21–24.

_____

_____

_____

_____

Reviewing 1 and 2 Samuel

22. From all that you've seen in 1 and 2 Samuel, how would you summarize the quality of David's service to God and His people in his reign as Israel's king?

_____

_____

_____

_____

_____

23. What particular truths about human nature come through most strongly in 1 and 2 Samuel?

_____

_____

_____

24. What particular truths about God come through most strongly in 1 and 2 Samuel?

_____

_____

_____

25. Remember again God's reminder in Isaiah 55:10-11 — that in the same way He sends rain and snow from the sky to water the earth and nurture life, so also He sends His words to accomplish specific purposes. What would you suggest are God's primary purposes for the message of 1 and 2 Samuel in the lives of His people today?

_____

_____

_____

_____

_____

26. Recall the guidelines given for our thought-life in Philippians 4:8 — "Whatever is true, whatever is noble, whatever is right, whatever is pure, whatever is lovely, whatever is admirable — if anything is excellent or praiseworthy — *think about such things*" (emphasis added). As you reflect on all you've read in the books of 1 and 2 Samuel, what stands out to you as being particularly *true,* or *noble,* or *right,* or *pure,* or *lovely,* or *admirable,* or *excellent,* or *praiseworthy* — and therefore well worth thinking more about?

_____

_____

_____

_____

_____

_____

27. Since all Scripture testifies ultimately of Christ,
    where does *Jesus* come most in focus for you in
    this book? In your understanding, what are the
    strongest ways in which 1 and 2 Samuel point
    us to mankind's need for Jesus and for what He
    accomplished in His death and resurrection?

_____

_____

_____

_____

_____

28. Recall again Paul's reminder that the Old
    Testament Scriptures can give us patience and
    perseverance on one hand, as well as comfort
    and encouragement on the other (see Romans
    15:4). In your own life, how do you see the
    books of 1 and 2 Samuel living up to Paul's
    description? In what ways do they help to meet
    your personal needs for both perseverance and
    encouragement?

_____

_____

_____

_____

_____

For the Group

You may want to focus part of your discussion for lesson 10 on the following overall key themes from 2 Samuel. How do you see these themes developing in chapters 21–24? And what other recurring themes have you noticed?

- God's covenant with His people
- Godly leadership
- Sin, repentance, and forgiveness
- Community and family

The following numbered questions in lesson 10 may stimulate your best and most helpful discussion: 4, 5, 6, 7, 8, 9, 13, 15, 18, 19, 20, and 21.

Allow enough discussion time to look back together and review all of 1 and 2 Samuel as a whole. You can use questions 22–28 in this lesson to help you do that.

Once more, look also at the questions in the margin under the heading "For Thought and Discussion."

1. Dale Ralph Davis, *2 Samuel: Out of Every Adversity*, Focus on the Bible Commentary Series (Fearn, Scotland: Christian Focus, 1999), 262.
2. Davis, 263.
3. Davis, 267.
4. Davis, 273.
5. Davis, 268.
6. Davis, 269.
7. *ESV Study Bible* (Wheaton, IL: Crossway, 2008), on 1 Kings 11:34-39.
8. Davis, 286.
9. Davis, 289–290.
10. *NIV Study Bible* (Grand Rapids, MI: Zondervan, 1985), on 2 Samuel 23:1.
11. Davis, 298.
12. Davis, 300.
13. Davis, 305.
14. Davis, 308–309.
15. Davis, 310.
16. Davis, 314–315; 317–318.
17. Davis, 315.
18. Davis, 320.

STUDY AIDS

For further information on the material in this study, consider the following sources. They are available on the Internet (www.christianbook.com, www.amazon.com, and so on), or your local Christian bookstore should be able to order any of them if it does not carry them. Most seminary libraries have them, as well as many university and public libraries. If they are out of print, you may be able to find them online.

Commentaries on 1 and 2 Samuel

A. A. Anderson, *2 Samuel*, vol. 11, Word Biblical Commentary (Thomas Nelson, 1989).

A. F. Kirkpatrick, *The First Book of Samuel* (Cambridge University Press, 1918); and *The Second Book of Samuel* (Cambridge University Press, 1905).

C. F. Keil, and F. Delitzsch, *Biblical Commentary on the Books of Samuel*, translated by James Martin, Biblical Commentary on the Old Testament (Eerdmans, 1956; available in various reprint editions).

Dale Ralph Davis, *1 Samuel* (Focus on the Bible, 2000) and *2 Samuel* (Focus on the Bible, 2002).

David F. Payne, "1 and 2 Samuel," *The New Bible Commentary* (Eerdmans, 1970).

David T. Tsumura, *The First Book of Samuel*, New International Commentary on the Old Testament (Eerdmans, 2007).

Hans Wilhelm Hertzberg, *I & II Samuel: A Commentary,* The Old Testament Library (Westminster Press, 1964).

P. Kyle McCarter Jr., *I Samuel,* vol. 8, The Anchor Bible (Doubleday, 1980); and *II Samuel,* vol. 9, The Anchor Bible (Doubleday, 1984).

Ralph W. Klein, "1 Samuel," vol. 10, *Word Biblical Commentary* (Word Books, 1983).

Robert D. Bergen, "1, 2 Samuel," vol. 7, *The New American Commentary* (Broadman & Holman, 1996).

Robert P. Gordon, *I & II Samuel: A Commentary* (Regency Reference Library, 1986).

Ronald F. Youngblood, "1, 2 Samuel," vol. 3, *Expositor's Bible Commentary* (Zondervan, 1990).

Historical Background Sources and Handbooks

Bible study becomes more meaningful when modern Western readers understand the times and places in which the biblical authors lived. *The IVP Bible Background Commentary: Old Testament,* by John H. Walton, Victor H. Matthews, and Mark Chavalas (InterVarsity, 2000), provides insight into the ancient Near Eastern world, its peoples, customs, and geography to help contemporary readers better understand the context in which the Old Testament Scriptures were written.

A **handbook** of biblical customs can also be useful. Some good ones are the time-proven updated classic *Halley's Bible Handbook with the New International Version,* by Henry H. Halley (Zondervan, 2007), and the inexpensive paperback *Manners and Customs in the Bible,* by Victor H. Matthews (Hendrickson, 1991).

Concordances, Dictionaries, and Encyclopedias

A **concordance** lists words of the Bible alphabetically along with each verse in which the word appears. It lets you do your own word studies. An *exhaustive* concordance lists every word used in a given translation, while an *abridged* or *complete* concordance omits either some words, some occurrences of the word, or both.

Two of the best exhaustive concordances are *Strong's Exhaustive Concordance* and *The Strongest NIV Exhaustive Concordance. Strong's* is available based on the KJV and NASB. *Strong's* has an index by which you can find out which Greek or Hebrew word is used in a given English verse. The NIV concordance does the same thing, except it also includes an index for Aramaic words in the original texts from which the NIV was translated. However, neither concordance requires knowledge of the original languages. *Strong's* is available online at www.biblestudytools.com. Both are also available in hard copy.

A **Bible dictionary** or **Bible encyclopedia** alphabetically lists articles about people, places, doctrines, important words, customs, and geography of the Bible.

Holman Illustrated Bible Dictionary, edited by C. Brand, C. W. Draper, and A. England (B&H, 2003), offers more than seven hundred color photos, illustrations, and charts; sixty full-color maps; and up-to-date archaeological findings, along with exhaustive definitions of people, places, things, and events — dealing with every subject in the Bible. It uses a variety of Bible translations and is the only dictionary that includes the HCSB, NIV, KJV, RSV, NRSV, REB, NASB, ESV, and TEV.

The New Unger's Bible Dictionary, Revised and Expanded, by Merrill F. Unger (Moody, 2006), has been a best seller for more than fifty years. Its 6,700-plus entries reflect the most current scholarship and more than 1,200,000 words are supplemented with detailed essays, colorful photography and maps, and dozens of charts and illustrations to enhance your understanding of God's Word. Based on the NASB.

The Zondervan Encyclopedia of the Bible, edited by Moisés Silva and Merrill C. Tenney (Zondervan, 2008), is excellent and exhaustive. However, its five 1,000-page volumes are a financial investment, so all but very serious students may prefer to use it at a church, public, college, or seminary library.

Unlike a Bible dictionary in the above sense, *Vine's Complete Expository Dictionary of Old and New Testament Words,* by W. E. Vine, Merrill F. Unger, and William White Jr. (Thomas Nelson, 1996), alphabetically lists major words used in the KJV and defines each Old Testament Hebrew or New Testament Greek word the KJV translates with that English word. *Vine's* lists verse references where that Hebrew or Greek word appears so that you can do your own cross-references and word studies without knowing the original languages.

The Brown-Driver-Briggs Hebrew and English Lexicon by Francis Brown, C. Briggs, and S. R. Driver (Hendrickson, 1996), is probably the most respected and comprehensive Bible lexicon for Old Testament studies. *BDB* not only gives dictionary definitions for each word but relates each word to its Old Testament usage and categorizes its nuances of meaning.

Bible Atlases and Map Books

A **Bible atlas** can be a great aid to understanding what is going on in a book of the Bible and how geography affected events. Here are a few good choices:

The Hammond Atlas of Bible Lands (Langenscheidt, 2007) packs a ton of resources into just sixty-four pages. Maps, of course, but also photographs, illustrations, and a comprehensive timeline. It includes an introduction to the unique geography of the Holy Land, including terrain, trade routes, vegetation, and climate information.

The New Moody Atlas of the Bible, by Barry J. Beitzel (Moody, 2009), is scholarly, very evangelical, and full of theological text, indexes, and references. Beitzel shows vividly how God prepared the land of Israel perfectly for the acts of salvation He was going to accomplish in it.

Then and Now Bible Maps Insert (Rose, 2008) is a nifty paperback that is sized just right to fit inside your Bible cover. Only forty-four pages long, it features clear plastic overlays of modern-day cities and countries so you can see what nation or city now occupies the Bible setting you are reading about. Every major city of the Bible is included.

For Small-Group Leaders

Discipleship Journal's Best Small-Group Ideas, vols. 1 and 2 (NavPress, 2005). Each volume is packed with 101 of the best hands-on tips and group-building principles from *Discipleship Journal's* "Small Group Letter" and "DJ Plus" as well as articles from the magazine. They will help you inject new passion into the life of your small group.

Donahue, Bill. *Leading Life-Changing Small Groups* (Zondervan, 2002). This comprehensive resource is packed with information, practical tips, and insights that will teach you about small-group philosophy and structure, discipleship, conducting meetings, and more.

McBride, Neal F. *How to Build a Small-Groups Ministry* (NavPress, 1994). *How to Build a Small-Groups Ministry* is a time-proven, hands-on workbook for pastors and lay leaders that includes everything you need to know to develop a plan that fits your unique church. Through basic principles, case studies, and worksheets, McBride leads you through twelve logical steps for organizing and administering a small-groups ministry.

McBride, Neal F. *How to Lead Small Groups* (NavPress, 1990). This book covers leadership skills for all kinds of small groups: Bible study, fellowship, task, and support groups. It's filled with step-by-step guidance and practical exercises to help you grasp the critical aspects of small-group leadership and dynamics.

Miller, Tara, and Jenn Peppers. *Finding the Flow: A Guide for Leading Small Groups and Gatherings* (IVP Connect, 2008). *Finding the Flow* offers a fresh take on leading small groups by seeking to develop the leader's small-group facilitation skills.

Bible Study Methods

Discipleship Journal's Best Bible Study Methods (NavPress, 2002). This is a collection of thirty-two creative ways to explore Scripture that will help you enjoy studying God's Word more.

Hendricks, Howard, and William Hendricks. *Living by the Book: The Art and Science of Reading the Bible* (Moody, 2007). *Living by the Book* offers a practical three-step process that will help you master simple yet effective inductive methods of observation, interpretation, and application that will make all the difference in your time with God's Word. A workbook by the same title is also available to go along with the book.

The Navigator Bible Studies Handbook (NavPress, 1994). This resource teaches the underlying principles for doing good inductive Bible study, including instructions on doing question-and-answer studies, verse-analysis studies, chapter-analysis studies, and topical studies.

Warren, Rick. *Rick Warren's Bible Study Methods: Twelve Ways You Can Unlock God's Word* (HarperCollins, 2006). Rick Warren offers simple, step-by-step instructions, guiding you through twelve different approaches to studying the Bible for yourself with the goal of becoming more like Jesus.

Encounter God's Word
Experience LifeChange
LIFECHANGE by The Navigators

The LIFECHANGE Bible study series can help you grow in Christlikeness through a life-changing encounter with God's Word. Discover what the Bible says, and develop the skills and desire to dig even deeper into God's Word. Each study includes study aids and discussion questions.

N A V E S S E N T I A L S

Voices of The Navigators—Past, Present, and Future

NavEssentials offer core Navigator messages from such authors as Jim Downing, LeRoy Eims, Mike Treneer, and more — at an affordable price. This new series will deeply influence generations in the movement of discipleship. Learn from the old and new messages of The Navigators how powerful and transformational the life of a disciple truly is.

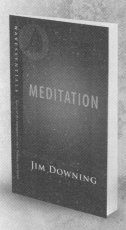 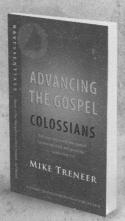 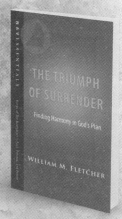